Noahide Laws

The *Final* Persecution to the Church

D1738739

Dr. June Dawn Knight

TreeHouse Publishers
www.treehousepublishers.com
Printed in the United States of America

TreeHouse Publishers
Dreams Come True in Our House!

TreeHouse Publishers
https://www.treehousepublishers.com/
Printed in the United States of America

DEDICATION

I dedicate this book to Steve & Jana Ben-Nun or sometimes known as Steve & Jana Benoon. I met them two years ago when COVID first hit. I was fresh out of Washington DC and heard about them due to their Noahide Laws teachings. I ended up meeting them and learned so much. This book contains all of their wisdom and knowledge from their research.

Thank you Steve and Jana for all of the years of hard work, suffering and research you put into this!

We know that Steve said he was in Chabad for 25 years and the CIA for 5 years. We truly respect your insight into this diabolical plan. We pray the best for both of you and your families.

Noahide Laws – The Christian Holocaust Coming
@2022 *What the World? Series*
7th Book in the *What the World Series* of **Books**

CONTENTS

1
What is the
Noahide Laws?

According to Chabad.org, the Jewish website, it states:

What Are the Seven Noahide Laws?[1]

The 7 Noahide Laws are rules that all of us must keep, regardless of who we are or from where we come. Without these seven things, it would be impossible for humanity to live together in harmony.

1. **Do not profane G-d's Oneness in any way.**
    a. Acknowledge that there is a single G-d who cares about what we are doing and desires that we take care of His world.
2. **Do not curse your Creator.**
    a. No matter how angry you may be, do not take it out verbally against your Creator.

---

[1] https://www.chabad.org/library/article_cdo/aid/62221/jewish/The-7-Noahide-Laws-Universal-Morality.htm

3. Do not murder.

    a. The value of human life cannot be measured. To destroy a single human life is to destroy the entire world—because, for that person, the world has ceased to exist. It follows that by sustaining a single human life, you are sustaining an entire universe.

4. Do not eat a limb of a living animal.

    a. Respect the life of all G-d's creatures. As intelligent beings, we have a duty not to cause undue pain to other creatures.

5. Do not steal.

    a. Whatever benefits you receive in this world, make sure that none of them are at the unfair expense of someone else.

6. Harness and channel the human libido.

    a. Incest, adultery, rape and homosexual relations are forbidden.

    b. The family unit is the foundation of human society. Sexuality is the fountain of life and so nothing is more holy than the sexual act. So, too, when abused, nothing can be more debasing and destructive to the human being.

7. **Establish courts of law and ensure justice in our world.**

    a. With every small act of justice, we are restoring harmony to our world, synchronizing it with a supernal order. That is why we must keep the laws established by our government for the country's stability and harmony.

As you can see, they sound like they could be a part of our Ten Commandments, but they are not.

Revelation 2:9 - I know thy works and tribulation and poverty (but thou art rich), and I know the blasphemy of them that say they are Jews and are not, but are the synagogue of Satan.

They are mostly Orthodox Jews who are making these so-called rules and calling them the Noahide Laws. They are seven laws given by the Talmud (oral tradition book). They will use these laws to destroy Christianity and take over the world. They do not like the fact that there is only one way to Heaven. I'm assuming that they feel that we have stolen their inheritance.

3

Jeremiah 3:8 - And I saw, when for all the causes whereby backsliding Israel committed adultery I had put her away, and given her a bill of divorce; yet her treacherous sister Judah feared not, but went and played the harlot also.

They do not like the fact that Jesus is the door and the only way to Heaven. There is no other way. There is only one covenant and its through Jesus Christ.

Revelation 3:20 - Behold, I stand at the door, and knock: if any man hear my voice, and open the door, I will come in to him, and will sup with him, and he with me.

John 14:6 Jesus saith unto him, I am the way, the truth, and the life: no man cometh unto the Father, but by me.

There is a group called the Orthodox Jews. They work at the United Nations everyday led by a man with last name of Cohen.

They are working towards global peace – a one world order. You can discover more about their UN goals at Chabad.org or Noahide.org.

On Noahide.org they explain this as, "There are seven laws, which are biblically binding on all humanity. They are prohibitions on idolatry, blasphemy (or the reviling of G-d), forbidden sexual relationships, theft, murder, lawlessness (the failure to establish courts and processes of justice) and the consumption of the limb of a living animal, associated with cruelty to animals. They are known as the seven Noahide laws. The reason for this name, is ostensibly because, although[1] six of the laws were commanded to the first person, Adam, the seven laws were completed with Noah, to whom the seventh commandment was given. Only after the flood, was it permitted to humanity to slaughter meat for consumption, and with this came the law prohibiting one to eat the limb of a living animal." [2]

According to Michael Hoffman, author of *Judaism's Strange Gods*, he describes the religion who sponsors the Noahide Laws as, "Orthodox Judaism is a religion of lies a tangled web of deceit compounded by duplicity and draft in guile.

We will never restore America's Christian roots, its constitution, or its Republic as long as Judaism can masquerade as a family values partner with patriots against

---

[2] https://noahide.org/prospectives-on-noahide-laws/

the forces of evil. Judaism is a religion founded upon the defiance and nullification of God's law."[3]

Mr. Hoffman's book is very eye-opening. He describes this religion as, "...the depravities of Orthodox Judaism, the religion which is the self-confessed ideological and spiritual heir of the Pharisees who persecuted Jesus Christ."[4] This means that this group is a Sadducee and a Pharisee. They are the ones who led to the death of Jesus to begin with.

The Fake Jews Who Act Like They are Evangelical or Pentecostal

I have been doing shows about how they will act like they are one of us and they are not. I did a show yesterday about a couple in Jerusalem acting like they are the two witnesses. I could tell within five minutes that they were Orthodox Jews and Noahide. There are many of these Messianic Jews on Christian Television as well that are undercover Noahides. You will even see them with the Noahide rainbow in there and other clues.

According to Hoffman in this book he says, "Certain rabbis are supposed allies of conservative Christians. Surely it must be a notorious fact by now, that Talmud-true rabbis

---

[3] Hoffman, Michael, Independent History & Research, Pg. 28, Judaism's Strange Gods, www.revisionisthistory.org

[4] Hoffman, Michael, Independent History & Research, Intro, Judaism's Strange Gods, www.revisionisthistory.org

have been luring Christians into their sphere of influence by posing as Biblical conservatives. Judaism is a form of social engineering of the *goyim* involving a multi-tiered system of statements that do or do not have a validity depending on which audience of percipients they are directed. To an audience of conservative, "family values" *goyim*, Talmudists will make statements upholding the Bible's standard on sex before marriage (abstention). Anyone who was to mistake these statements for Judaism's actual teachings on the subject would be foolish indeed."[5]

NOAHIDE LAWS AND FLORIDA

I have been watching Florida with Governor DeSantis. I believe he is a Jew himself. Also, when he first was placed into office, he took his staff to Israel. Texas did the same thing. Now, you see DeSantis working very close with the Noahides. It appears they are also grooming him for the White House or a bigger title.

They used him as an example in Florida as a "champion for freedom" so that he will be at hero status with the conservatives and Christians. However, it is a trap.

---

[5] Hoffman, Michael, Independent History & Research, Pg. 55, Judaism's Strange Gods, www.revisionisthistory.org

When I drove to Florida for a business meeting in January, the entrance into Florida on the interstate is focusing on evangelicals. The signs on the side of the interstate are about how their state is for pro-life, etc. They want Christians to move there. They are targeting them.

At the same time while he is acting like he is not wanting his people to be forced to take the vaccination, (I call it the V), he is giving them the other treatments like monoclonal treatments which are the same thing! Also, when you drive through the state you notice the increase in the infrastructure terribly! The checkpoint-charlies are awful! See my pics:

(5G Lights)

(5G Lighting systems that have internet, cameras and mics in there)

I call these checkpoint-charlies. They will call out the non-compliant in the future with LED screens, etc.

Notice the weird tall thing on the top

I also traveled to one of their smart cities and checked out their infrastructure. The truck weigh stations in Florida and all over the country are being converted into checkpoints for the lockdown coming as well.

NOAHIDE LAW KEYWORDS

I've noticed in the legal paperwork words that reflect these laws. There's only a few but you need to know what they are:

- **Natural or natural law** – They're meaning like going back to the foundation (Abraham/Noah)
- **Moral or Moral Code** – They feel they are superior in morals
- **Sodomy** – Although publicly they seem to support the LGBTQ community – you will learn when you see Jana's interview that they really do not. This is why I believe Milo called himself a Sodomite instead of ex-homosexual like normal vernacular. He is connected through his associations the Noahides.
- **Education & morals** – They are behind the educational system in America. Presidents for many years have signed the Education Day paperwork with the Noahides since George Bush. This is especially big in Florida with DeSantis. He is making all kinds of changes in Florida's education system based on morals.

Beware of the Hebrew Roots Movement

Part of the agenda in the Noahide Laws agenda is to corrupt the church and take them away from the foundation of Jesus Christ. They are using the New Apostolic Reformation leaders (NAR) to pull the church back into the Hebrew Roots. The problem is that they then lead them into the Talmud and other mystical, New Age teachings.

The Hebrew Roots movement are the ones who take the Christians away from faith in God to the legalistic way of the past. They begin going backwards and celebrate feasts, etc. You will notice over time that their flame goes out. It appears that way because they become so rigid. Especially when they go to sabbath route of worshipping on Saturdays. They're so about the law and faith goes out the window. Christianity is about faith. Jesus is out of the box.

Romans 3:20 Therefore by the deeds of the law there shall no flesh be justified in his sight: for by the law is the knowledge of sin. 21 But now the righteousness of God without the law is manifested, being witnessed by the law and the prophets; 22 Even the righteousness of God which is by faith of Jesus Christ unto all and upon all them that believe: for there is no difference:

23 For all have sinned, and come short of the glory of God; 24 Being justified freely by his grace through the redemption that is in Christ Jesus: 25 Whom God hath set forth to be a propitiation through faith in his blood, to declare his righteousness for the remission of sins that are past, through the forbearance of God; 26 To declare, I say, at this time his righteousness: that he might be just, and the justifier of him which believeth in Jesus. 27 Where is boasting then? It is excluded. By what law? of works? Nay: but by the law of faith. 28 Therefore we conclude that a man is justified by faith without the deeds of the law. 29 Is he the God of the Jews only? is he not also of the Gentiles? Yes, of the Gentiles also: 30 Seeing it is one God, which shall justify the circumcision by faith, and uncircumcision through faith.

The sad thing is that the people who are going back in their faith and hanging Jesus on the cross will miss out on the full destiny that Jesus has for them. They will never experience that glorious walk of faith.

Faith takes us to the highest heights that regular box religion will not. Faith takes you to the highest tower in New York City to see the view. Faith takes you to the White House with *$9 and a Suitcase.*

Faith takes you across the country in 36 states, 18,000 miles in 6 months in a car with a rod knocking, bald tires and 260,000 miles. Faith allows you to see God in such a miraculous way. It's an exciting life. Hebrew Roots is death. It is root to the Tree of Knowledge of Good and Evil. It seeks after knowledge more than the supernatural of God. Be careful Bride.

President Trump's Daughter
Ivanka and Jared Kushner

President Trump is right along this Noahide agenda. His daughter married an Orthodox Jew. We know that when Trump went in office that it was highly unusual that his family was able to travel all over the world and speak on behalf of the United States. They had no clearance. It is too weird. When Trump traveled, he often highlighted Ivanka. I believe he did this to show her as presidential material. I believe we may see Ivanka/DeSantis in 2024!

Here is a scenario I have in my head that could be a possibility:

Trump is forced to not be able to run (even though he tells the world he wants to – as usual).

Then the conservatives and Trump fans/worshippers are so disappointed that they will get behind Ivanka as loyalty to her father.

Then they will support all of her Judaism direction due to loyalty to Trump. It will be the perfect way to bring in the Noahide Laws 100% and have the church behind it!

Did you know that most of the Biden's administration is Jewish as well? Vice President Harris' husband is as well.

Trump is stacking the Republican Party with the America First vomit. Most of them are Jewish! They both are stacking the country with Jewish leadership. If not Jewish, then loyalists who are.

Noahide Laws in a Nutshell

The Noahide Laws is an agenda to kill the Bride. They want to get revenge for stealing their inheritance. This is the Freedom Farce root. They want to discredit Christianity, the United States Christian roots and our inheritance. They believe they are Jacob, and we are Esau. This is the Free-Edom story. I don't see it like that though. I see it as we are the Jacob (lineage to Jesus), and they are the Esau. They're trying to steal our inheritance.

Jesus is the only way to Heaven. He is the door.

FUTURE WITH THIS AND TECHNOLOGY

Pretty soon they will do predictive thought. They will judge you by either thinking negative about Jews, Noahide Laws or LGBTQ AGENDA. Just as they will be doing predictive crime, they will do predictive thought.

Dr. June Dawn Knight

2

Transcripts from News Shows, Interviews and Conferences

Over the years through my *News Today* shows and *Bride Time LIVE* interviews, I have gathered much information you need to know. This answers everything we need; the who, what, when where and how about the subject of the Noahide Laws. You will hear from people I consider experts in this subject.

This is very dangerous about the Peace Deal - Prepping for Noahide Laws January 2020 on WATB.tv

Dr. June - Bride. I did not understand the way that they did it on this.(The Abraham Accords in January 2020). I did not hear this from the president. Okay. So, when I heard that just now, it is very alarming, extremely alarming. There is no way this could not be the peace deal that we're all thinking of. First of all, the peace deal has to include the covenant with many. We know that they said that many nations are coming together in this covenant against what, extremism? And then I find out today. They actually did an Abraham Accord.

What The world? I've been telling you about this, about the State Department.

Dr. June - Remember I said that they had this department called *International Religious Freedom*, which they try to say that they're fighting for people to have religious freedom? But really, it's the ecumenical base. And they have a division of their department called the *Abrahamic Faiths Initiative.* This is the one world religion bride. I told you this before, but the Abrahamic Faiths Initiative is what the NAR has partnered with in this Hebrew roots movement. All of this has been doing this to pull people back to the roots, to Abraham and Noah's time, because they're going back before Jesus, which I told you yesterday. They want to get rid of Jesus and the New Testament. They want to get rid of the Christians.

Dr. June - So, let's listen to what the President has to say about this Accord. I'm in shock. Because they actually did it. The persecution to the church is about to be ramped up tremendously. And my heart grieves for all of us for what we're about to go through because of this covenant right here.

Trump: It will be known as the Abraham Accord. And I'd like to ask our ambassador, David Friedman, to please explain why we're doing and calling it the Abraham Accord.

David: Thank you, Mr. President. And congratulations to you on brokering this historic endeavor. Abraham, as many of you know, was the father of all three great faiths. He's referred to as Abraham in the Christian faith, Ibrahim in the Muslim faith and Abram in the Jewish faith. And no person better symbolizes the potential for unity among all these three.

Sky News: I'm joined now by the *United Arab Emirates, Minister of State for Foreign Affairs*, Dr. Anwar Gargash. Thank you very much indeed for being with us this evening. It's much appreciated. So, this has been quite a day. The UAE making this deal. What does it entail and why is it so important?

Dr. Anwar: Thank you, Jonathan. Good evening. It's been a great day. I think to start with. We have a clear commitment to stop annexation. So, the undermining of a two-state solution is something that has been dealt with so clearly with American help. We've been concerned, like many, many other countries, that the threat of annexing Palestinian lands, as will be the major, major threat to the prospects of a two-state solution. And through this deal, Israel is committed to suspend any annexation plans. And at the same time, we are committed to on the process of **normalizing our relations with Israel**, leading to diplomatic relations. I think it's an important step here. We don't really decide how peace looks like and how it should be. This is a Palestinian-Israeli issue.

Dr. Anwar - But I think what we have done by leveraging Israel's need to establish relations with the Arab world and winning this respite for a two-state solution, I think this is a win-win solution. I think the concern of, you know, the demise of the two-state solution has been an Arab and global concern. So, what we have really done is we have taken that off the table. The threat of a two-state solution is off the table. It will not be off the table forever. But clearly, we it's off the table currently. And we're hoping that this will encourage the Palestinians and the Israelis to go back to the negotiating table. Asking to do is very limited, Jonathan. What we really are seeking to do is to defuse the threat of annexation on the two-state solution. We have achieved that. We have never come and claimed that we will resolve this issue. This is up to the Palestinians and Israelis. But our role is really to defuse that sort of sword hanging on a two-state solution, which has been a concern for all our friends in Europe, in the Arab world. It's a very, very limited achievement that actually gives the prospects of a two-state solution much longer shelf life. Now it's really up to the parties to use that and to try and build on it.

Jared Kushner: What we saw was when the president rolled out his vision for peace, which we worked very hard on for a couple of years between the Israelis and Palestinians. We look forward to 180 pages of detail on how we can address the issues of the past, but also figure out how to move forward. *During that acknowledgment, President Trump was able to get Israel to agree to have a two-state solution with the Palestinians.*

My Thoughts About This Show

Notice how the gentleman from UAE kept making it a point that it was not the two-state solution? Notice also that he said they normalized their relations in this? This is code talk. They actually did do the final peace deal in January 2020. Jared ended the conversation by admitting they did. See the double-speak? The evangelicals who surrounded Trump tried to deny it was the biblical-prophetic event we were all waiting on to kick off Tribulation time. NAR was working lockstep with the United Nations to deceive the Bride and catch them off-guard. Here are a few examples:

Trinity Broadcasting Network
November 2020

TBN did a series to show the Christians it was not the biblical prophecy and presented the Abraham Accords Peace Deal as a good thing…

Tonight on Praise, a preview of the Abraham Accords. Look for episode one on Friday, November 5th. In the ancient history of the Middle East, a man named Abraham received a promise from God that he would become the father of many nations. The Bani Israel are the Jewish descendants of Abraham's son, Isaac, from his wife Sarah. The Bani Isma'il are the Arabic descendants of Abraham's son, Ishmael, from his wife's handmaiden Hagar.

From the house of Israel, the Jewish prophet Moses would be born, and the Torah would be written. Centuries later from the house of Israel, Jesus, the Messiah of the Christian faith would be born, and the New Testament would be written.

From the house of Ishmael, the Islamic prophet Muhammad would be born, and the Quran would be written. Through the centuries, the three religions of the Abrahamic faith have collided.

In no place more so than Jerusalem. With the fall of the Ottoman Empire after World War One, ancient nations were restored in the Middle East, including the state of Israel, fulfilling Old Testament prophecies.

And every US President since has tried with greater or lesser success, to build the alliances needed for a lasting peace. Recently, at an unlikely time with an unlikely group, led by an unlikely president, nations of the divided faiths of Abraham came together against all odds, and laid a foundation for peace that bears the name of their common father. -----The Abraham Accords -----[6]

My Thoughts on TBN

Isn't it sad how they tied all three together? They did not call out the idolatry of the other faiths. See, this is the problem. When you have ministers like John Hagee who tell the Jews that they can get to Heaven off their old covenant, then we have a problem. There is only one way to Heaven and His name is Jesus. He is the only door.

---

[6] https://www.tbn.org/specials/the-abraham-accords

Romans 10:9-10 - That if thou shalt confess with thy mouth the Lord Jesus, and shalt believe in thine heart that God hath raised him from the dead, thou shalt be saved.

John 3:36 - He that believeth on the Son hath everlasting life: and he that believeth not the Son shall not see life; but the wrath of God abideth on him.

John 14:6 - Jesus saith unto him, I am the way, the truth, and the life: no man cometh unto the Father, but by me.

Ephesians 2:8-9 - For by grace are ye saved through faith; and that not of yourselves: it is the gift of God

John 3:16 - For God so loved the world, that he gave his only begotten Son, that whosoever believeth in him should not perish, but have everlasting life.

John 3:3 - Jesus answered and said unto him, Verily, verily, I say unto thee, Except a man be born again, he cannot see the kingdom of God.

Titus 3:5-6 - Not by works of righteousness which we have done, but according to his mercy he saved us, by the washing of regeneration, and renewing of the Holy Ghost

John 6:28-29 - Then said they unto him, What shall we do, that we might work the works of God

Isaiah 53:11 - He shall see of the travail of his soul, and shall be satisfied: by his knowledge shall my righteous servant justify many; for he shall bear their iniquities.

Ephesians 1:7 - In whom we have redemption through his blood, the forgiveness of sins, according to the riches of his grace

Revelation 3:20 - Behold, I stand at the door, and knock: if any man hear my voice, and open the door, I will come in to him, and will sup with him, and he with me.

John 3:7 - Marvel not that I said unto thee, Ye must be born again.

Acts 2:38 - Then Peter said unto them, Repent, and be baptized every one of you in the name of Jesus Christ for the remission of sins, and ye shall receive the gift of the Holy Ghost.

1 Peter 1:23 - Being born again, not of corruptible seed, but of incorruptible, by the word of God, which liveth and abideth forever.

UN, NWO, Trump, V, Persecution
May 15, 2021[7]

I've been showing you the videos that has been coming from our State Department. I started calling these the Trump Fruit Stand. These are the statements that President Trump makes from his *Save America* or his *Office of the 45*. I'm going to begin to show these so you can see the fruit of what he's doing right now.

This is what he said today dated May 15th. He says "our country is being destroyed both inside and out. The presidential election of 2020 will go down as the crime of the century." He is still ranting on that. This is a readout from President Biden with Palestinian Authority President Mahmoud Abbas. This is dated today. He said, "the convoy of the US commitment to strengthen the US Palestinian partnership."

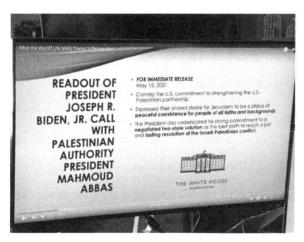

He expressed their shared desire for Jerusalem to be a part of a peaceful coexistence for people of all faiths and backgrounds.

---

[7] https://youtu.be/ESZHFRPGdGM

Now. I've been showing you, Bride, how all of the different faiths are going to have their headquarters in Jerusalem. **Jerusalem is going to be the seat of the beast**. This is where the One World Religion headquarters will be. I showed you the other day the press release from the Secretary of State where he talked about religious freedom, which is the cover that they have for it - where he talked about how religious freedom is going to protect non-religious people.

And he said it's going to protect people of conscience, which I've told you Bride already - **it means it's going to protect the LGBT.** So, we all know as well that **Israel is actually the greatest offender of God of the LGBT movement, because they have the headquarters in Tel Aviv.** It's in Tel Aviv, but they're actually **moving it to Jerusalem.** So, I have been reporting that it appears that the LGBT is trying to start a religion and trying to get rights. What we're seeing gathering in Jerusalem is the LGBT community and we see which we know they have great agendas and then all of the different religions.

The State Department announced that they are partnering in a multilateral agreement over all of this. And then we see this today by the **President declaring peaceful coexistence for people of all faiths and backgrounds**. This is him officially recognizing that Jerusalem is going to be the co-exist state.

The president also underscored his strong commitment to a negotiated two-state solution as the best path to reach a just and lasting resolution of the Israeli-Palestinian conflict.

Now we know that the Abraham Accords was a two-state solution. So, they are just continuing in that.

This is a readout of President Biden's call with the prime minister, Benjamin Netanyahu of Israel. This is also dated today. The president reaffirmed his strong support for Israel's right to defend itself against rocket attacks from Hamas and other territory terrorist groups in Gaza. The president shared his grave concern about the inter-communal violence against Israel. **He welcomed the statements by the Prime Minister and other leaders opposing such hateful acts and encouraged continued steps to hold violent extremists accountable and to establish calm.**

Bride, let me tell you, this is terrible on so many levels and let me tell you why. Since we just had the government come out and tell us that **we're now under international law.** And then you're going to tell us that all of these things that are happening over in Israel is going to result in them coming together in this big global agreement against extremist and to establish calm.

I see that as a persecution toward the church. Jerusalem is to be a place of peaceful coexistence for people of all faiths and backgrounds. And this is what he explained with Benjamin Netanyahu.

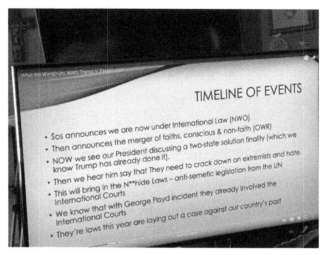

TIMELINE OF EVENTS

- Sos announces we are now under International Law (NWO)
- Then announces the merger of faiths, conscious & non-faith (OWR)
- NOW we see our President discussing a two-state solution finality (which we know Trump has already done it).
- Then we hear him say that They need to crack down on extremists and hate.
- This will bring in the N**hide Laws – anti-semetic legislation from the UN International Courts
- We know that with George Floyd incident they already involved the International Courts
- They're laws this year are laying out a case against our country's past

So, there is an agreement here with all of the leadership. Between the Palestinians. Between Israel and between the United States and listen to how dangerous this is Bride.

They all agree that Jerusalem is going to be the place for peaceful coexistence for people of all faiths and backgrounds.

And he also affirmed his support for a two-state solution.

Now what I want to explain to you is what I see, what I have picked up on through the news lately that you need to know about. Everything is escalating.

The other day, **the Secretary of State announced that we are now under international law, which is the New World Order.** They are not telling it through mainstream media or most of the Christian news organizations. Has anybody out there heard about this that's in the chat? Has anybody heard any of the other news organizations talk about what happened this week and the grave concern about it?

Then the next thing is then they announced the merger of faith, conscience and non-faith, which is the one world religion. Now we see our president discussing a two-state solution finality, which we all know Trump has already done that. **And then we hear them say that they need to crack down on extremist and hate.** I have already told you by the escalation of their terminology towards extremists and hate. Remember I told you some of the words they use like **colonialism**? You know, **white supremacy**.

This will bring in the Noahide laws Bride, anti-Semitic legislation. Listen to this. Anti-Semitic legislation from the U.N. international courts. This is me guessing, of course. But this is what I see this could lead up to. Because if you look at how they're announcing these things at the same time. While they're announcing about coming under international law.

And you'll see through today, through this broadcast, how they're already acting that out. They're going to use this opportunity **through the international courts** to come down on the church.

They're not going to say Christians. They're just going to use terms like, okay, it's international law. There will be no hate antisemitism. You cannot speak against Jews, which means you can say Jesus is the only way to heaven, etcetera, etcetera.

We know that with the George Floyd incident it led to the Black Lives Matter incident. They already involved the international courts. Do you remember that last year? **Their laws this year are laying out a case against our country's past.** I told you this, by the way, that they're writing stuff is like they are creating a case against America.

Now, I believe that they're setting us up for persecution. Persecution on a terrible level because they are building a case against our country, being a Christian nation. I told you about Trump's *1776 Commission*, and that had a lot to do with that. The deal that's happening right now with the cyber hacking of the oil. Okay. That I believe I don't know if it's fake or what, but because of that, just like with Israel, because of what's happening in Israel, they turn around and make all these laws when all these things happen. **With the cyber hacking, I believe that now they just announced today they have merged all of these different cyber organizations.**

They're getting all of these cyber people and everybody together as one. Because they're all going to be working together for global security. Do you hear what I'm saying?

They are saying that if we have an oil crisis here with a cyberattack, it affects everything globally. They're saying that everything that happens now is no longer one country. It is all the entire globe. So, they're coming together in all of these incidents. And I agree with Thomas, who's saying the banking system is next. Yeah. Which is the *Great Reset*.

So, what is going to happen for them to cause the unity of the banking system, you know? Now, I believe as well concerning the cyber part that this is rolling out the passport. I believe that that is working with that along with the RFID technology deal.

Now, as the president announces about the mask yesterday and the shaming thereof of the non-vaxxers, I believe all of this is escalating. At the same time, persecution is coming brought on a terrible level.

Now, Bruce Jenner, let's talk about Bruce Jenner and Trump a minute and the Republicans. How the Trump supporters can go along with that agenda. They ought to be ashamed of their self if they're Christians. I mean there's a lot of Trump supporters that are progressive that came over from the Democratic Party. I'm not talking to you. I am talking to the Christians. This ought to cause you to get on your face and repent and come out from among them. And then not only that, but you also got the mainstream media who says they hate Trump. They know what Trump's doing with Bruce Jenner. Why are they not wearing it out? Why are they supporting this agenda?

Why are they not blowing this up and saying, look what he did? You see what I mean? They're all together. It is a farce. This is the Illuminati vomit. It's all of them working together for the end goal. To destroy the American family and to destroy the church.

The Secretary of State speaking about the continuing atrocities and denial of humanitarian access in Ethiopia's Tigray region.

SOS: The United States is gravely concerned by the increasing number of confirmed cases of military forces blocking humanitarian access to parts of the Tigray region. **We also again call on all parties to comply with obligations under international humanitarian law.**

Dr. June: So, this is our secretary of state telling them you are transgressing the law. So, you need to come under and comply with the international laws.

SOS: The continued presence of Eritrean forces into ?? further undermines Ethiopia's stability and national unity.

Dr. June: Now, remember, Bride, that I told you the difference between stability and unstable. Okay. Whenever they say stability, they're talking about the U.N. agenda. Are they stable with the U.N. agenda or are they unstable? If they're unstable, means that somebody over there is not cooperating with the UN agenda.

SOS: We again call upon the government of Eritrea to remove its forces from Tigray.

Dr. June: This is from the United Nations News. Now, notice the logo here. I told you, we've already talked about this. This looks a lot like President Trump's logo.

UN: Civilian casualties climb as U.N. chief calls on all parties to immediately cease fire, cease fighting in Gaza and Israel. The UN chief called for mediation efforts to intensify and said the UN was actively involved in such efforts, which are also key to maintain the life-saving flow of aid to Gaza. The UN Humanitarian Affairs Coordination Office Osha also raised the alarm on Friday over the continued escalation of violence, noting that civilians on both sides were bearing the brunt.

WHO: The World Health Organization is calling for more UN control and authority. This is May the 12th. (Reading an article) - A prestigious World Health Organization appointed panel on Wednesday urged bold action to end the COVID 19 crisis, while also calling for the UN agency to be given greater authority to respond more quickly to future threats.

Dr. June: That right there should really cause you to pause, Bride. Because the World Health Organization is telling the U.N., hey, we need to have more control over the whole world.

Now what I want to remind you of Bride is that they are saying this after the meeting with the United States and the Secretary General of the United Nations. After that meeting is when the Secretary of State went live and told everybody that **we are now agreeing to be a part of the universal world and we are under international law. We're going to honor international law**. After the United States is all in. So, I don't know what agreement they signed at the U.N.

I don't know what they've done to make this new world order official. **But they are now about to crack down and take more order of the world**. That's exactly what they're saying right there.

WHO: Our message is simple and clear. The current system failed to protect us from COVID 19 pandemic.

Dr. June: I have been reading their documents, and I know for a fact that they have said they are going to honor the World Health Organization in the *American Rescue Plan*.

I'm telling you right now that our country is under the UN.

I know I'm the only one out there saying it, but I'm just telling you, Bride, you need to do your research because I'm showing you the proof.

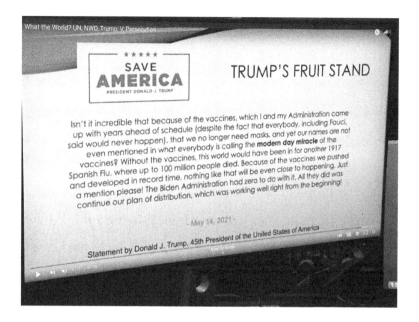

My Thoughts:

Notice in this story how it was confirmed by the Secretary of State that we are underneath the United Nations. We are honoring International Law. It can't be any plainer than that. Also notice in the graphic above how President Trump is bragging about his role in the vaccine agenda.

Jana Ben-Nun Speech at We are the Bride
2020 CHOOSE Conference

Jana: I think we need to review what Noahide laws are and why we are afraid of them. Let's see, why we do not agree, and I don't think we should as Christians agree. And is it a Sharia law or is it the Noahide law that is supposed to be on a watch for or both?

Right. So, are you familiar with ministries that say the Noahide laws are, okay? They're harmless. They're no big deal. They're godly. They're out of the Bible. Did you? Are you familiar with ministers? There is several of them out there who are saying Noahide laws are nothing bad. They're good laws and we should embrace them, and we shouldn't be afraid of them. Right. **Well, I have a totally different view on this.** And after we review what Noahide laws are and what is their actual problem with them, you make up your own mind. You make up. You make your own decision. **I also would like for you to understand that President Trump is part a huge part of a Chabad organization.** He is part of the entire cult that's called Chabad. And I say cult because it is a mega cult that took over the world. **In my eyes they are the head of the snake.** And why do I say that? There is a group of Jews in Israel, in New York, and all parts of the world that disagree with Zionism.

Jana: Did you know that? They're Jewish rabbis. They're still part of Judaism. I will explain to you why Judaism is not a correct religion and **Judaism has nothing to do with Christianity**. We will talk about this. But those rabbis are still Judaic. They believe in Talmud. They embrace Talmud. They embrace Zohar. But they're against Zionism. They don't believe that Jews should be in the land of Israel right now. They are pro-Palestinian. They want equal rights for Palestinians. That you just don't hear about those people because the media will never show them. And when they are in front of the presidential building protesting, they never show it. They never show it.

But there are people who are Jews who dislike Zionism, and they say it's actually against Judaism. How bad is a specific cult or branch of Judaism that was started by Russians? Russian rabbis. And you might be familiar with Rabbi Schneerson. OK. He is the historical figure. He died in 1994, I think. **But he's the one who kind of put in motion the whole Chabad organization and spread of it and proselytizing of it all over the world.** And they have put Chabad, they have put their feet in almost every government of the world. **And they are the ones who want Noahide laws for the Gentiles.** Now the rabbis who are against Zionism also study Talmud and they know about Noahide laws, because they're Talmudic. They're not out of Bible, their Talmudic laws, but they do not believe that they should be forced on us right now, that the Jews should be taking this into their own hands.

Jana: They wait on the Messiah, and they think Messiah is the one who is going to who is going to do it. I still disagree with that part of Judaism, but I would just want you to know that **Chabad is a specific cult that I call radical.** Very radical, like you heard of radical Muslim, radical Muslims. **These are very radical Judaic. And it is a cult.** It is a criminal cult, a very criminal organization that is involved in sex trafficking, organ trafficking, money laundering and all kinds of sins and crimes you can ever imagine. **And I want you to know that our president is part of this.** As good as he sounds and as everybody wants to be, you know, pro-Trump, just please understand. **Behind him is Kushner and Ivanka.** Did you ever vote for Kushner or Ivanka who immediately came as his adviser, was his own son in law? There is part of the Chabad cult OK. They went before he was elected.

They went into they went to pray to Schneerson to his grave so president trump can win the election. This is called necromancy. They did not pray to almighty god. They prayed to the dead Rabbi. That Rabbi. Okay. So, I want you to know the powers that are behind Trump. And when we talk about politics, Democrats, as I said, is a secular form of Judaism. It's communism. That's part of the Jewish movement. **The far-right Republicans are a part of Chabad.**

Jana: Chabad is also in Russia and China now and practically every government of the world, and **they are all connected together. When American government speaks of your enemies as Iran, Russia, and China as enemies, it's natural. It's not true.** They're not our enemies. *You need to understand because Putin, Trump and China are all connected through Chabad.* So, if you understand this basic, then you see. Who are we really fighting? We are fighting the enemy. **And there is a Hegelian dialectic in place.** It's a part of divide, divide and conquer strategy, meaning they're going to divide you. You hate each other. You fight each other so they can conquer your nation. That's basically what's going on. And Chabad is at the head of it all. So, Noahide laws, just basics, I was just basically going to go through basics. They are not biblical laws. **They are spelled out only in the Talmud as seven laws.** We have Ten Commandments in the Old Testament. We have two commandments in the New Testament by Jesus. Love your God and love your neighbor. These are the two commandments of Christ, but they are like ten puts together, right? Right. The first four, I think, is love your God, and the next six would be love your neighbor. So, Jesus kind of put them all together, and he said that within you is you get reborn from inside, you transform to his image. Then you are born again, and the laws are on your heart that are within you immediately.

Jana: Right, you do to others as you want them to do to you. So, the law of love is actually the law of Christians. It's the law of love. Not complicated, very easy, because if you in Christ, it's simplicity, it's extremely simple. **And in that basic simplicity is what Jews actually hate about Christianity.** It's extremely simple. All right. Noahide laws that are also known as natural laws. If you go to this website right here, http://www.naturallawassociation.org/agenda.html, we're going to go through this website. So, you understand when Natural Law Society, you will be surprised there is Schneerson and Noahide laws and rainbow. Okay, so when they speak of natural law, they speak of Noahide laws. The law of ethics. They're also called it law for peace and safety. And they call it also justice. **I forgot to put it in anything in the name of justice, morality, peace and safety, ethics, and natural law**. So, they kind of dress it up with all of these words so you don't even know their meaning, **Noahide Laws**. Now there are seven of them, but Noahide laws have many sub laws. Yes, there are only seven and they seem like they're godly, but they have many sub laws, and you know where the problem lies? It's not really in the laws, because we live in a law system. We have laws now. Can I drive 90 miles an hour? You know what the problem is with these laws? Who has the power of interpretation? How are they interpreted and who interprets them? Is it pastors? Is it Christians? No, it's the rabbis. **The power of interpretation lies with the rabbis.** And this is where the problem comes in. Okay, so there are laws for the Gentiles. Jews have 613 laws. Gentiles had only seven. Come on, Gentiles. You can't keep seven laws. You can. All right. According to Judaic beliefs, they are mandatory for salvation of Gentiles, **meaning that you cannot enter the world to come unless you submit to Noahide laws according to Judaism.** We will check out the website at the end so you can see. Now this is from Chabad.org. So, you understand how they list these laws. The Mitzvot of non-Jews, the Mitzvot means commandments or mitzvah. The commandments.

Number one, carry out justice an imperative to pursue an end for social justice and a prohibition of any miscarriage of justice. Sounds innocent. We all want justice. We don't blaspheme God right. No idolatry, which prohibits the worship of any human or any created thing. Also prohibits the making of idols and involvement with the occult. This necessitates an understanding of the one God of Israel and his nature.

Number four, no illicit intercourse - this prohibits adultery, incest, homosexuality, bestiality, according to Torah definition. Number five, no homicides, or no murder. Prohibits murder and suicide causing injuries. Also forbidden. No theft. Prohibits the wrongful taking of another goods. And don't eat a limb of a living creature. Promotes a kind of treatment of animal life. It also encourages an appreciation for all kinds of life and respect for nature as God's creation. So, when I read you these laws in a simpler way, by the way, you need to know **the rainbow is the symbol for the Noahide laws**. We are coming back to rainbow as a concept. Right?

Simply, they have a different order on this one. It's no idolatry, no cursing God, don't murder, no illicit relationship, don't steal, no animal torture, and uphold justice. What's wrong with any of it? Anything?

Brock: On the surface it looks good.

Jana: Nothing wrong with it. No problem, right? Now I am going to go through Kabbalah online, Kabbalah.org (now societyofsouls.com) and some of the interpretations of these laws.

Jana: So, we are going to go through this together so we will understand why Noahide laws are a threat to Christians according to rabbis' interpretations. In Kabbalah, the seven commandments that are equivalent to the seven lower Sefirot, the ten Sefirot through which God made the world and men are divided into three intellectual attributes **wisdom, understanding and knowledge.** In Hebrew, it's chokmah, biyn, and da'at. And seven emotional ones. Kindness, my beauty, eternity, glory, foundation, and sovereignty which I will explain soon.

The three intellectual attributes are associated with the Jewish people who provide the legal and spiritual interpretation of the seven laws to the descendants of Noah. Each law parallels one of the seven emotional Sefirot. I'm going to stop here and explain to you something. The three intellectual attributes are associated with the Jewish people who provide the legal and spiritual interpretation of the seven laws to the descendants of Noah.

Descendants of Noah is you, *the goyim*, the Gentiles. They have what kind of rights? Legal rights and spiritual rights to interpret these seven laws. Nice sounding laws to you. Right? Now, something that maybe you didn't catch. Do you know what Sefirot is?

Jana: Sometimes it sounds so innocent, and people are so happy to be on a friend bridge with them. But once you learn what is it, what they really mean, then you find out you have been deceived. Okay? The three intellectual attributes are associated with the Jewish people. The highest Sefirot, the ones that are divided into three. You see in the beginning attributes, wisdom, understanding and knowledge in Hebrew chokmah, biyn, and da'at. These three are the Jewish people.

They have the knowledge, the understanding, and they are intellectually higher than Gentiles.

This is why the interpretation lies with them. **They're the ones who are going to decide How are the seven laws interpreted for you**. Do you understand me? Okay, now I'm going right now and I'm coming back to this. I'm going to the Sefirot tree. This is Kabbalah tree.

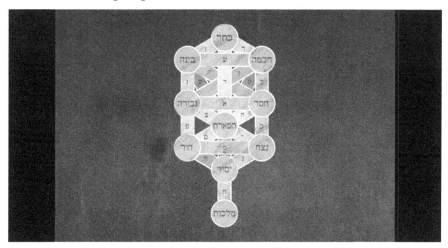

Now, this is a Kabbalah tree that is real. That's in their Kabbalah literature with the snake through it, you have to understand this snake represents their messiah. Holy Serpent. Okay. All right, let's go back. These are the ten Sefirot of the Kabbalah. Do you see the biyn, da'at, and chokmah, understanding, knowledge and wisdom? Do you see those? Those represent the Jews. The lower ones represent the Gentiles, meaning you are hierarchically under them. The kathar. You know what kathar is? Corona Crown.

Brock: What is this on the website?

Jana: Yeah, but no, there is this. Kabbalah is everywhere now.

They're teaching it openly and freely. Corona, the entire thing that's happening right now. It's not pandemic. We don't have any pandemic. If we had a pandemic, you would know it by now, because maybe half of you here wouldn't exist anymore. Look around. Everybody is alive and well. And if they just left us alone, we would go about our normal life. And nothing would be wrong. Businesses wouldn't be closed. There would be no lockdowns. Corona set everything in motion for them. For them, the kathar at the top represents above that kathar. Shaddai is the name of their God, the Jewish God. It's not Father of Jesus. I just need you to know that it's Shaddai. That's the name of their God. This is the Kabbalah. There is a crown that sets in motion entire process of their redemption.

Jana: This is why you are seeing what you see. This is why after lockdowns, you heard that the rabbis were secretly meeting the Messiah. It's because it's all about Jerusalem and who they're going to bring there for their Geulah. You know that Geulah is redemption for tikkun olam. Geulah, you know, I'm not good in Hebrew, but tikkun olam is their term for repairing the world. **They want to be the ones who repair the world.** They're going to create a chaos, poverty, famine and all kinds of stuff and tribulation for Gentiles. **So, you will be looking for answers and they're going to have them.**

Jana: They will come with the answers for you. You need Noahide laws. We have the tech. See, we can cure the cancer.
Oh, you have no water, but we can create water out of air. Did you

know that this is a technology that Israel has, and they want to offer it to the world? But hold on. They're not just going to give it to you. First, you're going to lose your water. Then they're going to have the solution. But there is a price to pay. So, you have to understand what kathar is and how it's Corona virus, how it's connected to the entire process of what's happening right now. And its Kabbalah unleashed. Kabbalah unleashed right now upon the world. And this is what's happening. Let me go back. All right. So, we learned about the status Gentiles are from the lower class. They are the higher the Jews. And they have a legal and spiritual rights of interpretation. Idolatry.

The law of idolatry is one law that I'm afraid of for Christians. Why? Well, let's read. Idolatry and blasphemy correspond respectively to nature and hope, which are often paired together as the two supports of faith. Idolatry is a violation of divine rulership and blasphemy of divine love, since God's rulership and his love are inseparable, each in turn facilitating the other. So, two of these two commandments supported in hands each other, God alone, is to be worshiped directly without any conjoining or intermediary, and he alone desires and here spread out of his love for all mankind.

Jana: The problem comes in when you hear that God is to be worshiped without intermediary. **They mean Jesus.**
You cannot have Jesus who is the one mediator between God and man. Jesus. This is going to be prohibited.

You won't be able to worship Jesus.

You might keep him in your dictionary somewhere that he was a man. According to Talmud, he was a man. And we will learn about this. How they talk about Jesus. He was just a man. According to Muslims. He was a prophet. According to a lot of religions in Christianity and Christian cults, he was an angel. Michael Archangel, Jehovah's Witnesses, Unitarians. Jesus is not divine. He was just the prophet. Right. Okay, so this type of idea will be all right.

Believe or not, when Trump signed for religious freedom, that means that you can still be called Christians. But the time is coming, you won't be able to worship Jesus because according to Noahide laws if Jews take over and they are taking over because you see Trump and Chabad.

Chabad is a number one organization that Schneerson started that he is preparing the nations for Noahide laws, and Chabad. **Kushner is a Noahide loving Jew, meaning Noahide law promoting Jew and Ivanka.** Do you think Ivanka converted to normal Judaism? No. Cult like most deviant criminal cause there is Chabad organization.

So, you will not be able to worship Jesus because according to Noahide laws, to pray to an intermediary is prohibited and they are into in Jewish interpretation.

Jesus Christ is not God, and you are never to worship Him. **So, it is a very dangerous law for Christians.**

Now, when it comes to blasphemy, on one of the sub laws, you have to understand that Jews are considered divine people in Judaism. **They're considered very special chosen people, spiritual people with a special right, that you, as Gentiles, never will have.** And if you go against a Jew, you're going against God himself according to Judaism.

Do you remember when Trump signed antisemitism laws? That's preparation for the law of the blasphemy.

When antisemitism laws will become criminal for you to say and defend your faith and say what I'm saying right now. I committed blasphemy because I went against the divine people and to hurt the Jew is to hurt God according to Judaism. This is why, when he signed antisemitism laws, I knew immediately what it means. They are preparing the infrastructure for a future Orwellian Noahide World.

A lot of people are asking me, what is this with eating a limb of an animal or whatever? And as you can see in one of the things there, they explain that you are not to torture animals and to be kind to animals. I have no problem with not torture.

I don't like torture of animals. Do you? Nobody does. Okay. But when you are signing on Noahide laws and you're putting your name down, it's equivalent to taking a blank piece of paper and signing a name on it, your name on it, and say, I accept.

Jana: And then later they add to that paper whatever they want. This is signing Noahide laws. You know why they can change it any time they can change interpretation on it on a whim. Rabbis can do that. Look what they say here what eating a limb is. Eating a limb from a living animal corresponds to the Saphira of the salt associated with the reproductive drive. The link between eating and sexuality is well known. The eating of living meat fosters the purely rapacious aspect of both eating and sexual relations. It adds to the desire for purely exploitative sexual relations which resemble eating. Since such food contains the actual heat of life which arouses selfish passions, sexual spaciousness and cruelty of all kinds are rectified by abstaining from living meat as defined by the Torah. This, in turn, inspires gentle and respectful practices such as those directed toward maintaining the environment. Maintaining the environment. Agenda 2030 anyone? Agenda 2030 is connected to the Noahide laws. Yeah, they're going to tell you how much sex to have, how to have it, how many kids you can have, how many resources are you going to use. Soon, they're going to outlaw gasoline. There are going to carbon free world by 2050, but by 2035, it's going to be only one third. That means that if you want to drive your old car, that uses gasoline, it will be impossible to get gas.

Jana: Or are you going to be heavily taxed because you drive it? There are about to get rid of fossil fuels. They are decarbonizing the world. Did you hear everything? Maintaining the environment, how much you eat, how you have sex, basically eating a limb from a living animal can mean anything. To them, they can reinterpret it to whatever they want to. Now, at the very end, I'm going to show you how Israel is a leading nation in creating us food from the worms, which will be a future food and protein for the Gentiles. Because you will not be eating meat, you will not be eating. They are changing even agriculture. This is why we are having coronavirus. It brought so many attacks on our food supplies. How are you going to eat in the future? This is all from Chabad or Kabbalah online. These are my sources on the topic. So, a functioning judicial system.

> *Now, of course, maintaining justice is another very big problem in our high laws because there is a decapitation that is mandated by the rabbis.*

Jana: If you if you break any of the seven Noahide laws, you're going to be killed by decapitation. This is according to Talmud and according to Maimonides or Rambam, which is a 13th century Jewish scholar that our Congress has his picture right there in the United States. And he is Noahide promoting. Jewish scholar Rabbi who said that the Gentiles have to die by decapitation if they violate any of the Noahide laws. And United States Congress has his picture on the wall.

A functioning judicial system corresponds to the lowest Saphira of the strength, the lowest one is motherhood, which rules in supremacy but is selflessly devoted to public service. This is the responsibility of good government. Our sages, sages are rabbis, our sages state what comes to the world through the delay of justice, the perversion of justice, and a teaching of Torah, not in accordance with the Jewish law. When both Jews and non-Jews can learn the Torah without distortion of its halachic or Jewish legal meaning, the true peace becomes possible. I hope that you can understand what they are saying that even you have to be taught by Jewish rabbis, you have to be taught Jewish ways and a Torah, because without that, no peace is possible. This is why you saw in Washington all the Jewish symbols and all the Jewish things and come back to the rainbow. That's the justice for you. This is sickening.

Brock: Now the churches have changed their songs to Rainbow songs.

Jana: Oh yes. Because you see this infrastructure has been prepared for a very long time. Brock And they have all of these. Who does the who is selling the people out, the so-called pastors, these mega ministries who have signed up on that road with them for power, for money, you know, whatever they are promised, they're going to be very disappointed because in Jewish law, Gentile is never equal to a Jew? Never. I mean, you're always a slave. So, is that's what they want? They will get it.

This includes recognition of the principle that Jews can be judged only according to Torah law, no matter where in the world, and that non-Jews in Eretz Israel are considered according to the seven laws by the Jews there with no sovereign jurisdictions of their own. Did you hear that? No sovereign jurisdiction of your own as Gentile. The Complete Guide to seven Basic Laws can be found in Encyclopedia Talmudic under the Ben Noa. Philosophical understanding is available in seven laws of Noah. I am giving you all this from Jewish sources. I'm not making this up. This is from their own sources. I mean, I just read their websites and I own Zohar and I own the Talmud and I own their book of law and where I found out how they view Gentiles.

Jana: All right. This is in the Talmud. Now, when you have a Talmud, you know how a Bible has books? 66 books about Talmud also have its own little sections. And each book in a tablet and Talmud has its name. One of the names of the book is Sanhedrin. **So, in a book of Sanhedrin, chapter 57 A, it says one additional element of greater severity is the violation of any one of the seven laws subjects the Noahide law to <u>capital punishment by decapitation.</u>** There is a Jewish lawyer, I think by name of Lewis and Lewis husband and wife team. And they have been lobbying Congress to allow decapitation as the most human form of capital punishment in America. And it passed, and they defended it on a base of Talmud. Yeah. And they and Bush even had dinners with them. They had. Yeah, yeah, of course it passed. They will not tell you what's happening.

I found out that most of the time they have no idea what they're preparing behind our back. And everything they're assigning is basically one piece of a puzzle that fits into all of this agenda.

Jana: Like years ago when Trump signed anti-Semitic law. That's part of that. That's part of this thing. That means that you cannot defend your Christian faith.

You're going to have to be Judeo-Christian whether you want or not.

But we are going to talk about what Judeo Christianity is. This is in one of their books, **Omar Muhammad in chapter nine from Chabad, the daughter, a gentile who transgresses these seven commands, shall be executed by decapitation.** For this reason, all the inhabitants of Shechem were obligated to die. Shechem kidnaped, they observed and were aware of his deeds, but did not judge him. A Gentile is executed now, **and on the basis of the testimony of one witness and the verdict of a single judge.** No warning required relatives may serve as witnesses. However, a woman may not serve as a witness or a judge for them. So, patriarchy does come from Talmud. I'm not going into this. It did creep into Christianity from the Judaic beliefs, because Apostle Paul, even though you're going to tell me right now, he said, women keep silent. We are misinterpreting what Apostle Paul was saying but look at this. How many witnesses do we need? According to the Bible, Old Testament law? Two or three.

The Gentile just needs one witness. According to Judaic law. Jews cannot be executed or tried if family member comes to complain about him or tell on him.

Jana: For a Gentile, it can be your mother, sister, father, children, anyone. So, let's say that your, I don't know, son or daughter and teenagers get mad at you. I don't know. It will never happen. Right. Or whatever you understand. Like child in the school says that you pray to my daddy, pray to Jesus in a closet or whatever. I'm just making stuff up right now out of my own, you know, like what can happen if you are a Jew, your family member has no power to come and be a witness against you. **If you are a gentile, it can be your family member**. *Jews always gets a warning, not a Gentile.* No warnings for you. So how do you like this? Do you like to be on a friend bridge? Because I dislike this very much. And this is a deception that is these pastors are putting us into. We need to know we have a right to know what they teach in our synagogues. This is Sanhedrin 59 a to communicate anything to a goy (gentile), about our religious relations would be equal to the killing of all Jews. For if the goyim knew what we teach about them, they would kill us openly.

Jana: Isn't God the God of justice? What's wrong with Noahide laws? There are deceiving you because they're not telling you how they're interpreting them in rabbinic circles and Talmud. So, they're deceiving you. And they know that they cannot tell you the truth upfront because if they did, what would happen? Right.

Do you think that there would be so many Christians happy to be friends on a bridge with the Jews? By the way, when you go, and you are in a friend breach with the Jewish rabbis. When Jewish rabbis is invited to Christian Church to speak about prophecy, it happens now all the time. Do you think that friendship goes both ways? Like. Rabbi, you tell me how Isaiah 53 is interpreted in synagogue, and I will tell you how Isaiah 53 is interpreted in our congregations. Do you think that's what happens? What do you think happens? **It's a one-way street**. It's a one-way street. It's my way or a highway. You need to know that. **That's the friendship. It's my way or the highway**. They will never allow you. They will tell you have no right of interpretation because prophets were Jews. We gave you the Old Testament. You are to learn from me. That's their attitude. So, this is your friendship with the Jews? Be careful. They will not accept your interpretations. Who knows? Israeli Bible 365 Anyone? Do you know that Christian churches are promoting it?

Dr. June: Yes, it's horrible.

Jana: TBN is promoting it. Pastor Paul Begley is promoting it. Christians are buying this Bible crazy.

Steven: You think this is the Bible to put in schools that Trump talks about?

Jana: I don't know about Israel 365. But listen, this Bible - Pastor Paul Begley had Rabbi Weiss. And he has him as a guest. He promotes the Bible, and he says to the Christian people, there are some very awesome commentaries in this Bible. You need to buy this Bible. You need to read the commentaries. Do you know what's in these commentaries? They are written by rabbis. All of the messianic prophecies of the Old Testament that apply to Christ. They're applying to the Jews. It's not about Jesus in that Bible. It's about the Jews. Well, how do you think they interpret Isaiah 53 the messianic prophecy? It's all about the Jews. Their divine. They're the answer to our problems. They're the light of the world. Did you know in these commentaries it says that **Jews are the light of the world**, and that Bible does not include the New Testament, and it's been sold in Christian churches. It's the only Old Testament. There is no word Jesus in it, no name Jesus, not even Yeshua. Wow.

Jana: And they say in commentaries, the **Jews are the light of the world** and Christian pastors are promoting this, Bible. Who is the light of the world? Jesus is the light. Jesus. Since when are the Jews the light of the world? Well, this is the thing that I cannot understand. And these are men pastors doing this. So please wake up and wake your neighbor up. And it's either that you're going to be a Christian or just turn your back on him but admit that you did. Don't keep saying name Jesus. Let's go back to Noahide laws.

Some people say it's not really dangerous, blah, blah. Look, there is a public law 10214 congress.gov. You can go there. You can read it over here. I don't know if this is okay. Down here, you see a tracker. You see the tracker on the bottom. Introduced, passed House, passed Senate to president. What does it say? That it became a law. It became a law. It's on congress that gov. People say public laws are not real laws. Who do you what the real laws are? Why are we having this in public? Let me ask you this.

Jana: Do you know what law brought us as a part of United Nations? It was a public law. Public law brought us to as a nation. We are under United Nations. It was on the public law only. **So Noahide law is a public law.** That's what it is. And if our Constitution does not exist anymore, which it doesn't, how is our nation governed? By what? By executive orders, legislations, and public laws? That's exactly right. Because they can do it any time because they prepare the infrastructure for it. First of all, it has no business in there. And all Christians of this country should be going in front of the White House and saying, get it out, get this out, or you are selling us out. That's the truth. **It's hard to read, but it says to designate March 26, 1991, as education the USA, where that's when it was signed into law.** Whereas Congress recognizes the historical tradition of ethical values and principles which are the basis of civilized society and upon which our great nation was founded. Whereas these ethical values and principles have been the bedrock of society from the dawn of civilization when they were known as the Seven Noahide laws.

Whereas, without these ethical values and principles, the edifice of civilization stands in a serious peril of returning to chaos. Do you realize what they just said? They said that these are the ethical values that our nation was founded upon, and we need to return to those values.

Jana: Otherwise, we will have chaos. You need to return to the original rainbow. That's the Noahide laws. Alright, this is from the United Nations - uniting the United Nations with seven Noahide laws, diplomats, delegates, emissaries gathered at United Nations headquarters for one people, One World Conference. Think about this one people. One World. Globalism. One World. New World Order. United Nations. New York. June 10, 2013. On the heels of the Lubavitcher Rebbe, which is Schneerson 19 members of the UN Diplomatic Corps, UN press officers and other officials gathered at the UN headquarters in New York to learn how the seven Noahide laws must play a role in international efforts for world peace. They just read to read the wording; they must play a role in international efforts for world peace. What are they doing now? Peace and safety. That's all you hear, right? Yes. **On this day, people from all over the world gathered on behalf of the laws of Noah, said Rabbi Yaakov Cohen, head of Institute of Noah Code, which sponsored the conference.** Their observance is required so the division of the United Nations to have a settled and civilized world filled with economic justice and righteousness will prevail. They always dress it up in nice, beautiful world. **It's economic justice and it's righteousness.**

Jana: Well, that's very deceptive. Other speakers at the event included:

- Carter Gore, president of the Booker T Washington Business League.
- Richard Dawson, director of Dawson Associates International, who insisted that all Jews are obligated to teach the seven Noahide laws.

In addition to prohibiting idolatry, the Noahide code forbids blasphemy, forbids sexual relations, murdered relationship, forbidden sexual relationships, murder, theft, cruelty to animals. It also commends its followers to implement orderly practices of justice, just decapitation. **The Institute of Noahide Code is a *UN accredited NGO* dedicated to spreading awareness of the seven Noahide laws, which all people of the world are obligated to follow.** You are obligated to follow. It takes its guidance from inspiring vision of the Lubavitcher Rebbe. Remember, that's how they called Schneerson. **This is who Kushner is - Lubavitcher Rebbe Schneerson.**

You know you have a rabbi and then you have a rabbi, then somebody rabbi. In Jewish circles that is like divine figure. They are from a dynasty of rabbi. I mean. **By the way, Kushner considers Schneerson the Messiah.** Yeah. **Jews had many messiahs.** Did you hear us? Well, they prayed to him. Some of them believe they will still come back. **He'll be reincarnated in the Messiah. Like whoever the Messiah will be, He will be reincarnated Schneerson.**

That's what they believe. And do you know Sabbatai Zevi? Anybody heard of him? Okay, well, he was one of their messiahs.

Jana: You know how much Jewry believed in it? 50% of Jewish people embraced Sabbatai easily as the Messiah in a history. **And those are the ones who are financing and promoting homosexuality and transgender movement because they believe that through immorality and sin, the redemption will come.** So, they had to **pollute nations into horrible immorality.** And that's Sabbatai. And frankly, Sabbatai was their messiah. That's still that branch. It has many branches. How bad is another one? They are the moral ones. They're going to fix the sabotage. And whatever sabotage did, the cabal is going to fix it. **They're going to give you moral laws now to fix all that.** It's very complicated in a way. If you really study this, it's almost like your head spins and you are like, what on earth is that? This comes out of psychotic satanic mind. This is not normal.

Jana: March 11-13, 2007. Very important event happened. Christians have no idea. Catholics have no idea what happened. **Commission for Religious Relations with the Jews.** The Delegation of the Holy Sea Commission for Religious Relations with the Jews. And the Chief Rabbinate of Israel's Delegation for Relations with the Catholic Church. Bilateral Commission meeting happened and within this meeting they have signed. And if you look at this document, it's online, it's open to your research.

You will see bunch of bishops signing on that side and a bunch of rabbis on this side where it says **Jewish tradition emphasizes the Noahide covenant as containing the universal moral code, which is incumbent on all humanity.**

Jana: This is the Catholic Church signing the Noahide Laws with the rabbis. Now, the recent development was that the Holy Seer or whatever he is that Pope, he gave up his title of Vicar of Christ instead of Christ. That was for a reason. They signed on the No Child Laws, and he signed cooperation with Chief Rabbinate of Israel. And that was the event. There is a paper official document on online you can go check out.

Jana: American government. Russian government. Chinese government. South American government. Czech government. European government. All governments have signed on to the Noahide laws, Chabad is in all of them. **They're cooperating together for this one world, one piece, one world.** And the WHO represents Christianity, even though it's a past the Catholic Church, how all the evangelicals went on, the Catholics, you know that, right? You know how they all went on the back to the mama? Well, they all went back. And why was this happening? Everybody thought, well, it's going to be the Antichrist. He is. I mean, he's the Antichrist. There are many Antichrists. There's not just one Antichrist. There's many. **Well, pope is the Antichrist. Always was. Each one.**

Vicar a person who acts in place of another

Jana: Even his name, Vicar of Christ. The word vicar means instead. So, he says he's instead of Jesus, he's the pope, right? Okay. But why was the old evangelical signing going back to mama? Well, look what mama did. He gave up the title of Vicar and he signed up with the Chief Rabbinate of Israel for the Noahide Laws. Isn't that some suspicious activity? Isn't that okay? Trump Signs Noahide Laws on anti-Semitism. Bill. These are the two. On Antisemitism Bill. Who was right there behind him? Was it Pence? **It was Kushner. Did you vote for Kushner? Where did he come from? Where did he come from? Pits of Hell, he came from the head of a snake. He's a Chabad Jew, and he works very heavily for whatever Chabad vision is, and they are the ones promoting Noahide laws. So, this is Trump for you.**

Jana: You will be surprised what you find. Education Day 2018. Now, you know when. When Presidents were signing these Noahide laws, right. It was not all 50 states. They were here. This state sign or that states sign on. Right. Guess what happened in 2018? All 50 states. All 50 states did a proclamation. Noahide laws. Beginning with President Carter over this collective and individual responsibility to education. **They're going to do it through education.** That's why they are redoing education system. Is proclaimed each year on a day that corresponds to 11th day of Jewish months of Nisan four days before Passover anniversary of birth of Lubavitcher Rabbi Menachem Mendel Schneerson of righteous memory.

Jana: This is done in respect to the rabbi's tireless work spearheaded spearheading this national focus on education along with the towering personal example his life and teachings provide to direct and apply this educational emphasis. All 50 states persistently 2018 40th Anniversary of Education Day. The President of United States signed the traditional declaration of rabbi's birth as education sharing day, as did the governors of all 50 states in the Union. And when you go on that website, each proclamation with a golden star or whatever seal, it's right there. You can look up your state. Oh, so they all sold you out. Christians. It's so sickening. Now they say, how moral was Schneerson? And he's into education. What a great person he was.

Jana: This is what he taught. And non-Jewish soul comes from three Satanic spheres, while the Jewish soul stems from holiness the Chabad Lubavitch Rabbi Menachem and Schneerson. **He was the one who was teaching, and they are teaching Jews in synagogues, Chabad synagogues, that they are the light of the world, they are the chosen, and they are from the three highest Sefirot that I showed you.**

And the Gentiles are a separate species.

I'm not kidding you. You are the Neanderthals. You are a separate species from the lower Sefirot, and they are divine.

And you just never even can achieve this. You never can. You are just different species. Can you believe this? Turn this around. What if I was telling you here right now Jews are from different species. They are like Neanderthals are lower. They can never be spirit. They need us to tell them, can you be? What would I be? That would be hate speech, wouldn't it be? I'm a real anti-Semite. I'm like, really? I would deserve to be accused of hate speech. That's not what I'm saying. I'm telling you; this is what they say and teach about you. But Christians don't complain. They have lobbies like ADL. If you say anything against Jews, oh, they go nuts. It's all over. You're anti-Semite. We are anti-Semites. I ask you, do you have any lobbies, Christians, where you watch out for who hates you and Gentiles? No, you don't.

Jana: No, you don't. Nobody's watching out for us. For you. Nobody. Excerpts from the Lubavitch Rebbe shekels about Noahide. This is what he taught, how he was teaching and encouraging that they need to embrace Noahide Laws. He's the responsible one. And remember, he's their messiah. **He will be incarnated in the coming Messiah.** And they do his work, Kushner and Ivanka. The main service of this generation is to go out to the final war of the goals, to conquer and to **purify all Gentile countries such as that and kingship will be Haitians**.

So, they believe that they have to conquer Gentiles and purify them.

Our efforts must be geared to the final days in purifying and clarifying ourselves, in influencing the Noahides, to accept our God given destiny, which will cause the nations of the world to come before God and give honor to His name with a true and complete redemption through our righteous Moksha speedily and truly in our days. This is how he was teaching. So, you can see what he was saying. How Jews have to influence Noahides. **Noahides are basically Gentiles or descendants of Noah, which is Gentiles in their eyes.** With regards to the seven mitzvot or seven laws. The time has come to prepare the world for Moshe. This includes making it a settled place through spreading the seven laws, influencing non-Jews to keep their mitzvot.

Jana: The seven Noahide laws will assist our task of making the world into dwelling place for God and help bring about the arrival of Messiah. **One of the things that Chabad believes that has to happen for Mashie to rule and reign is the fact that Gentiles will be transferred into Noahides.** That's one of their beliefs. **And these are the beliefs of exact sect or code that Trump is part of.** So just be aware of that. The speeding of the true and complete redemption depends on this. The dissemination of seven Noahide laws and all of these sources are cited if you want to go see them when you go to Chabad.org, it's all about Schneerson and you can study this for days and months and you can see for yourself what all this is about. I did that work. Guess what? It's tiring, horrible, disgusting.

And once you really realize what's happening and then you can't open people's eyes, then I get so frustrated that I say I'm about to give up. Because I don't know how else to tell you in these critical times when nations are challenging one another and violence is increasing in unbelievable manner, the Jews have the power to bring about peace in entire world. Ideally, a Jew should stand proudly before the Gentiles and explain to them the seven Noahide laws emphasizing that they should be carried out not because they appear to be logically sound, but because God commends them.

Jana: When a Jew carries out mitzvot with pride and non-Jew stands in all of him and hence will not consider war. So, these are the teachings of Schneerson the Rambam. Remember who Rambam is? Congress has his picture on the wall. Maimonides. Remember? No, I wasn't decapitation. The Rambam uses the expression Lakoof to forcefully influence all inhabitants of the world, to accept nor hide commands forcefully. Although obviously one must do this in a pleasant, gentle, and peaceful way. It still must be done with persistence. If you have already tried several times, try again. Nevertheless, we frequently see that although people are sometimes spoken to five times, they do not change until they hear it a sixth time. They're going to keep doing this. This is this is how they think. Sorry to say that is necessary to protest against those who have the attitude and are voicing the opinion that they simply could not be bothered and that they have no time for convincing the citizens of the world to observe the seven Noahide laws.

Jana: So, I really recommend I'll recommend to you some websites today. Talmud says the Talmud said Jesus was along with Balaam and Titus, one of the three greatest enemies of Judaism. It says it in a book of Gittins 56 B 57 A So in Judaism, Christianity and Jesus is considered enemy. So, when they start speaking of friendships and bridges, this is like putting oil and water together when they don't mix. The New Testament confirms that the Pharisees considered Christ demon possessed, right? We have it in New Testament, John 8:48 A charlatan empowered by the Devil. Matthew 12:24 A Deceiver. Matthew 27:6 a Blasphemer in. John 10:36 And having unclean spirit in Mark 3:30, this is what our Bible says that the Pharisees thought about Jesus. That's how they were teaching about Jesus, who was a charlatan, who was a deceiver. He was demon possessed, right? Do you think that these Pharisees changed? The Talmud says he was a bastard son of adulterous Mary. That's in Book of Sanhedrin 1 of 6 B, He was hanged on the on the eve of Passover because he was a sorcerer, an apostate, in a book of Sanhedrin. Talmud 43A, He was a fool who fell down and worshiped a brick. I don't know. Sanhedrin, 67A. He was executed by stoning, burning, decapitation and strangling. They have four different ways how they killed. And that's what Talmud teaches. You know, it's not true. But this is how they explain it to the to the little Jewish boys in synagogues.

Jana: At three years old, every Jewish boy starts their Talmud education. This is what they tell them about Jesus. Jews are encouraged to lecture against Christ, and Christ is in hell. Wallowing in boiling hot sacrament. According to Talmud, the

Talmud recommends persecution of Christians. **Christians are heretics.** It's in a book of about Azaria. Their apostate is in a book of Sabbath 8:116. Christians may be legally thrown into a pit to die. Christians deserve death for observing the Sabbath, even though they observe the Noahide laws. And studying the Old Testament. Yeah. **And under the Noahide laws, you will be only allowed to study what they allow you to study**. You cannot just pick what you want as a Gentile. **Christianity is an unforgivable sin.** Seducing Jews to idolatry. According to Judaism, it's unforgivable sin. So how are they making these bridges? And this is what their theology is. Does it make sense? **The testimony of a Christian is unworthy to be admitted to a Jewish court.** Jews are forbidden to return a lost article to a Christian. The Jews should rejoice. Dress in white. Eat and drink and be merry at the death of a Christian. **They should hate a Christian without utmost hatred and consider him an enemy.** This is what they teach. But they don't tell you the truth because they're doing bringing all of this **false peace and Jewish order by deception.**

Jana: And of course, they have to deceive you. The Zohar, another of their sacred books. It says The Zohar sanctions killing of Gentiles, including Christians. Take the life of a Clinpath. Clinpath is another name for a Gentile and a Christian and kill them and you will please God, the same as one who offers incense to him. Does it remind you of radical Muslims? Because it does mean the people of the earth are idolaters and it has been written of them.

Let them be wiped off the face of the earth. When these shall be exterminated, it will be as if God had made Heaven and Earth on that day. At the moment, when the Holy One blessed behave, you exterminate all *goyim* of the world. The Lord alone will appear great on that day. It is certain. Our captivity will last until the princes of the Gentiles who worship idols are destroyed. In the palaces of the fourth heaven are those who lamented over Zion and Jerusalem, and all those who destroyed idolatrous nations and those who killed people who worship idols. You have to understand why that's important because **Christianity is considered idolatry in their eyes.**

Jana: A visionary book published in 1932 by Jewish Talmudic scholar Michael. Here I have that book. I have three copies of it. And every everywhere I go, I have that book because I studied it and highlighted it several times. Michael Hager gave Jewish Utopia is the name of the book where they actually wrote out all of their plan. It describes the brave new Jewish world, he says, when a Jewish one world ruler messiah comes, he will enforce Judaic monotheism. There will be no room for the idolatrous, and that's Christians, because Christians are considered idolatrous. Only those who are convinced of Israel's divine purpose of the world in the world will be welcome to join Israel in the building of an ideal spiritual life on Earth. Israel, the ideal righteous people, will thus become spiritually masters of the world. This is in that book by this Jewish author, rabbi, scholar. Before the Messianic Era begins, in general, the people of the world will be divided into two groups.

The Israel tic and non-Israel tic take the former will be righteous. They will live according to the wishes of one universal God. **All the other people, on the other hand, will be known for their detestable practices for idolatry and similar acts of wickedness.** They will be destroyed and will disappear from Earth before the ushering of the ideal era. **So, I just want to let you know that their plan is to really clean the earth of idolatry.**

Jana: And in their eyes, Christianity is idolatry. Just be aware of this plan. Let me just move on to. To refer to Christianity as Judaism. Christianity is oxymoron. I have said that many times, and I'll say it again. It doesn't go together. In no way. We will see why. It's a very basic redemption, which is tikkun loam in Hebrew, in Jewish mind, represents the idea that God will hand over the entire world to the Jews. **They will rule the world through Judaism and Sanhedrin, and the Gentiles will have to be Noahides, and they will have to slave the Jews.** Judea Christianity. If you look up Judeo Christianity, it tells you about a history on how this term even came up. The term Judeo-Christian first appeared in a letter from Alexander McCall from England. He was a preacher, which is dated October 17, 1821. So, 19th century. The term in this case refers to Jewish converts to Christianity. So, you can see evolution of the term Judeo Christianity. At first Judeo-Christian was a Jew who believed in Jesus, so they called him Judeo-Christian. That's not what it means today. The concept of Judeo-Christian ethics or Judeo-Christian values in an ethical, rather than theological or liturgical sense, was used by George Orwell in 1939, along with the phrase the Judeo-Christian scheme of morals or

Noahide laws. **Any time you hear the word moral, morality, be scared.** The phrase Judeo-Christian entered the contemporary lexicon, the modern lexicon at the standard liberal term for the idea that Western values rest on the religious consensus that includes the Jews.

Jana: And during late 1940s, evangelical proponents of the new Judeo-Christian approach lobbied Washington for diplomatic support of the new state of Israel. So Judeo Christian values, as they're known today, this is how they evolved. **The 1970, Jerry Falwell, he was a preacher. Some of you might know him, popularized the term Judeo-Christianity. He made that term popular. He called to return to Judeo-Christian values. He popularized the term among Republicans and said those values are the <u>foundation of America.</u>** He called for unconditional support of state of Israel. Christian evangelical right started to support Israel as a result. And until then, most Protestants supported plight of Palestinians. So, before all of this started that <u>the Christians actually felt for the oppression of Palestinians, but that actually dwindled away, and they started to support the oppressors.</u> And I'm not even going into that area, because if you knew what they're doing to Gaza, what they do to these people, it's an open-air prison. They're doing experiments on them of all kinds. They're controlling their food and water. I'm not going into that. But horrible. Criminal acts against humanity have been done on these people. And some of them are our brothers and sisters in Christ. And sadly, Christians support the oppressors. **Ethics and theology of Judaism greatly differs from ethics and theology of Christianity.**

Jana: Yet the term Judeo-Christian is a common place and people repeat and use this term automatically without thinking. You say I'm a Judeo-Christian. Really? Well, what does that mean? Explain.

Because you are either Judaic or you're Christian.

You can be both. Okay. Christianity versus Judaism. Just some basics. Jesus Christ is the Messiah and God in flesh agree. He died on the cross to redeem us from sin. The salvation is one free gift to mankind, based on faith in Christ. Well, Judaism. Let's see what Judaism is. Jesus was just a man and as a son of a whore and is boiling in excrement in hell. That's what they know. That's how they're taught. The true Messiah is yet to be revealed. Salvation is based on obeying laws and performing rituals as well as submitting to rabbis. Okay. So Judeo Christian. Yeah. Oxymoron Christianity. Jesus Christ. The head of the church. The church consists of believing Jews and Gentiles.

When anybody tells you are replacement ideologists, they are targeting you. They're targeting you. They are using psychology on you by calling you labels. False labels. No such thing. There is no such thing. They are replacement ideologists. They replace Jesus with themselves.

They are saying that they're light of the world, Jesus is the light.

Jana: They replaced Christ with themselves, and they are projecting their sin on you because you speak the truth of Scripture. The Church consists of who do we say? It's only Gentiles. No, God was so kind. Then, even after rejection of his son, he opened the arms and he said, if you receive him, he has opened arms. **Church consists of remnant of Jews and believing Gentiles, remnant of believing Jews, remnant of believing Gentiles.** And that is the teaching of New Testament. And no, ma'am. No, sir, it's not replacement theology. So, anybody accusing you learn how to defend yourself, because I have met so many Christians, so afraid of that title. Are they going to call me replacement here? I'm not a replacement theology. Of course, you're not. You just speaking the truth of scripture. **They are the replacement theology, and they project their sin on you.** That's psychological manipulation called projection, and they use it, and you need to learn what's happening so you can defend your faith, refuse it, say no, I am not a replacement theologist. Okay, Again, Jesus Christ, head of the church. The Church consists of living Jews and Gentiles. The wall of partition is removed. We don't say Jews are less or they are animals. Wall of partition is removed in Christ. We are all one. There are no lesser humans. Chosen nation is a spiritual believing nation. In Judaism, they believe they are a different species from Gentiles. They are on a higher spiritual plane.

They are a priestly chosen nation, while Gentiles are lesser humans who originated from lesser evil plane and must be submitted to and instructed by Jews.

Jana: So. Very different. Now, I don't know what that is. Genesis 12 How many times you heard our blessing that blessed you. Our curse. Curse. Those who are blessed, those who bless you all, those who curse or curse him, that curses you. That's the. Yeah. Genesis 12:3. That is another thing that they use to. It's a twisting of scripture and twisting of scriptural interpretation to make you support the state of Israel and the Jews. That scripture. Now, I have a full teaching on this, and at the end I'll show you when I get online, I'm going to show you where to find it, because that Scripture is fulfilled in Abraham Seed, singular, which is Christ, and that promise belongs to those who are in Christ. And this is the teaching of the New Testament. This is the teaching of our apostles. So, bring such teaching to church and interpret it. To base it on physical flesh of a race is absolute. I don't know what to call this, but it's horrific. Yet out of the pulpits of these pastors, this is what they say constantly to brainwash the people. And Christians do not understand their own Bible and interpretation of their word. They don't because any preacher is screaming it. I will stand up and leave and write him a letter.

Jana: They believe that Sanhedrin has jurisdiction within the land of Palestine or Israel. Okay? And outside of it, they believe they actually have jurisdiction. Sanhedrin has a jurisdiction over the nations.

Now, look, I'm not a Holocaust denier. Did 6 million Jews die? What if it was 6,000,500? What if it was 5,999,000? Well, you can't say 5,999,000. You can't say that because if you say that, Israel has power to extradite you to the state of Israel to be tried in a court. Did you know that? If you are European. Yes. Yeah. All Germans? No, it's 6 million in Czech. It's 6 million. Exactly. It's not 5 million and it's 6 million because we don't want to go to Israel to court. They have the power to extradite you. Look, what *Tom?* will teach is that they have jurisdictional powers over the nations, and the nations are handing them this power. Who do you say? Why the Czechs can be extradited? Why German people can be extradited? Who gave Israel this power? German government did. Yeah. So do you see they give the power to the beast. Who identified the beast? Who did? Jesus. Jesus identified it. What did Jesus say? It's very simple. Jesus said, if they persecuted me, they would persecute you. Now, who is they? Who is they? Yeah. **Well, who persecuted him? The Sanhedrin. And who is giving power to the beast? Trump. Definitely**. Well, and all the governments do, right? So, Christians do. All these Christians waving flags going, Trump. Trump? Yes. Knowingly or unknowingly. But they do. **They are handing the power to the beast**. Right. But Jesus told us he identified. They did it to me. They will do it to you. That is so powerful. Let me give you some resources. And I'm at the end. Noahide.org/article. You can read that for your own education on research. How was she? Joseph will be killed in battle. They want Gog/Magog battle because Christians are thinking this fulfillment of prophecy. But you see, you don't understand Jewish prophecy.

They're actually self-fulfilling their own prophecies and they are begging for war so they can bring the Messiah because they have got to have the Gog/Magog and they're most by Joseph, I told you about the two messiahs there is Moshe and Joseph has to be killed in a battle so there are self-fulfilling. They're artificially bringing about all of this, just like **Corona is artificial**. This is like a play like we are in a movie. **We are in the movie.** Yeah, we are in the movie. Once you find out actually what's happening, your brain stops and you're like, Wait a minute. I mean, are you serious now? I'm pulling back on you. I do. I don't mean to do this, but I really. Are you serious? They're playing a movie where idolatry will be destroyed. That's asknoah.org.

Jana: Now they want you have to understand they're not going to openly tell you this right now and they're going to deny this because what do you think they will just tell you that? It's something that you have to research on your own, what you're getting into. Trump is signing Noahide every year. Do you know that? They were on the lockdowns, and he still found the time to sign the Noahide laws on Education Day. Oh, well. And do you know there is a website called ifamericansknew.com on that website tells you how what they do to Palestinians during lockdowns secretly quietly. No name on the bill just bill passed $38 billion to the state of Israel.
Americans were losing jobs. Middle class Americans shops were closed. Hairdressers couldn't go cut the hair and feed their kids. But they silently signed $38 billion to the state of Israel. Now, let me tell you something.

What Trump needs to repent of if he is a Christian. The Bible says that you have an obligation to take care of your own first. Take care of your own first. Lockdowns he blames on Democrats. Hey, Republican states were locked down, too. Middle class lost jobs, too, and their businesses. If he is the president right now and all of this is happening, do you think it's going to change in November?

Jana: Well, he's president now. Listen to me. If this corona pandemic, lockdowns, and all of these lies were happening in Europe, Brazil, Cuba, you name it, it would be everywhere else, but not in America, because we are the land of the free and our freedoms are number one. And you know what? All of these health officials have no power because constitution is number one first, right? Then I would vote for Trump. I would say yes. Yes. And we would tell people, come to America, come to America for safety because we have Constitution, we preserve it. What's happening here? People don't look different than in Europe or they are muzzled, submitted. They lost jobs. They can. What happened to this woman the other day? She got arrested. Is there any difference between America and UK and Australia? No. So why would we vote for Trump? Or anybody that doesn't matter right now is no time to go vote for Jesus. Because you know what? We got to vote for heavenly government. I'm just giving your resources. *Israel 365 news dot com Sanhedrin blesses Trump Calls President Trump to Uphold the Seven Noahide Laws.*[8]

Jana: But you know what church and state together is, right? Well, Israel in 2014, 2014, Benjamin Netanyahu met with the rabbis of Israel, and he promised them that he's going to make Israel a Talmudic state and a Talmud is going to be a legal code in a state of Israel. **And he said it's going to happen when America puts embassy to Jerusalem.** Wow. Yeah, it's actually on my previous conferences. I have shown the proof you can Google it. Well, it happened. And who did this? Trump. So, Trump. Trump, right? Yeah. But anyway, what I want to tell you, Israel is not democracy. Israel is theocracy. Church and state will be together. Sanhedrin will rule. And it's a religious state. This is something that our constitution shouldn't ever, ever allow. Because if you put state and religion together, this that equals tyranny. You know, I am for religious freedom. I am not against Jews having synagogues. I am for religious freedom. **Have your synagogue teach what you want, but do not tread on me.** Yes. I want converts to Christ from heart and free will, not by force. So, basically, this is what my what ideology or whatever is. That's what did I do here? All right. Remember what I said about eating worms? I'm thankful to Celeste for what she gave me information back then. She, by the way, she does not agree with me on Noahide laws, which I am very surprised.

Jana: And this is why we had to separate. So, I can't call her on again because she goes directly against our research on our Noahide laws. And again, I'm not telling you here, but to believe or not. I'm giving you, my research. You research it yourself and make up your own mind.

Jana: But she did say in one of our interviews that they are going to attack our food supplies and are going to give us worms to eat. And I was like, so disgusted because I want to vomit or even think about this. Right? So, let's see what that one says here. Israel's food tech scene experiment with insects and computer designed sweeteners. **By the way, Israel is leading the world in AI. What is AI? Artificial intelligence.** Give me a definition of artificial. Thank you. Thank you. Virtual. Not real. Fake, right? Fake intelligence. Think about this. There are leading fake intelligence. You know what? They're setting up their kingdom. Earthly kingdom as rebellion to the true kingdom that is already set up. And they are doing it through fake technology. Jesus and his miracles. He didn't need technology. He doesn't need artificial intelligence. Jesus could walk through a door or wall, right? He can multiply fish and bread. He can feed the hungry. He can raise the dead. There was no need of artificial intelligence. **What they are doing is they're trying to imitate God's kingdom as a rebellion, to establish true kingdom of God through fake, through fakery.** Yes, yes. Do you agree?

Dr. June: Yes, I want to tell you about the favor that you're talking about. What is happening is with the luciferin kingdom. The reason they're doing the Internet of Things. Yes. Computer chips and everything which they want in humans. They want them in the animals. They already have an animal, but they want them in equipment like your you know, your appliances and all that. Yes. Satan cannot see all. Yes, God is all thing and all knowing.

Yes. So, he needs these computers. He is everywhere with this technology of this watch energy so that he can see everything. It's artificial.

Jana: Yes.

Dr. June: The beast is what is AI.

Jana: Right. And who leads it is state of Israel, by the way. They are the leaders of it. And they own the tech, and **they own surveillance technology**. *And they are the ones who are responsible for surveilling the world.* And everywhere in America now setting up surveillance, it's Israel Tech. You know, Deborah Tavarez, I was with her on the phone 1:00 last night. So, I'm so tired. I had to get up at 6 a.m. to come here. But I would want I was still talking with Deborah Tovar, and she was telling me, Jana, I'm doing this research and to my shock, I'm finding out everything is about Israel. She says, it's all out of Israel. I love her. Yeah, I mean, she's a researcher. So, let's look at this food thing. I'll end and we can have a break. Israel's food tech scene. This is not only the food of the future, but also the agriculture of the future and growing. Each company CEO said livestock is not sustainable. Sustainable Development Agenda 2030. Sustainable Development Agenda Livestock is not sustainable. You're not going to have chickens in store very long. Yeah, forget the chicken parmesan dinner. Okay? Yes. Now, it's not sustainable to grow a cow, chicken or even fish.

Jana: It still has a lot of issues taking up a lot of space, a lot of water, environmental issues. Insects are the answer. Insects, the larva, tasting, the larvae are blanched, milled and dried with the fat separated as an oil, the company hopes to sell four cosmetics. The remaining powder, the company says, is 70% protein, 12% minerals. The mix is very good. It's a whole protein. The bioavailability of the minerals is very high, Mr. Grandage said. In terms of sustainability, it has low greenhouse gas emissions, and we are using very little of water and land in a practice and hardly any waste because we are using 100% of the lot of it. The powder is being trialed as an additive to baked goods and energy bars and the company is planning to build a factory in Thailand. But it has a major investor, that Israeli company, that they're going to have there you know, anyway, the food of the future are the worms and the insects. So, and Israel is a leading company of Israel are leading in this in this 2030 agenda. So, and surveillance agenda. It's all Israel. Wow. Yeah. Because they are friends with Russia and China. By the way, I know that you think that all you know there are our friends. **But no, they're actually friends with Russia and China and they are dumping the U.S.A., say they don't need U.S.A anymore.** They only used us. I mean, and Benjamin Netanyahu did say the Christians are useful idiots. That's the words out of his own mouth. And anyway, I have given you my research, how I see it and how I understand it, understand all of this based on study of the New Testament history of Jesus and what he told us, who his enemies were, and knowing Judaism and their beliefs, what they teach on the inside, that they don't tell you on the outside, and they will deny to your face because they wage war with the deception. And we are in a war. Yes. So, and the war and we are the enemy. So, I just wanted you to all know this. I know I'm not very liked by many. So, if you put this in YouTube, I will be called anti-Semite. I don't know how safe this is, even for June's ministry. So, I don't know. You need to pray over this if we really should put this out. Okay.

Steven: That's a little bit too late.

Dr. June: I one of the questions that they had is about the Jews, about the Noahide laws is what about when you talked about the hierarchy on the Kabbalah tree and how the Christians are the low man on the totem pole and the Jews are higher? What about the Jews? They get saved.

Steven: What about the drop down? You don't drop down as low as a Gentile Christian.

Steven: Drop lower. Yes. Okay. All right. That's a Jana question. She knows about that. See, if you're Jewish and you become a Christian, then they consider you no longer Jewish. But you still have both. The Jews view that their soul is still considered higher than a Gentile. Wow. If you're a homosexual Jew, you're higher than a Gentile. Yes.

Dr. June: Wow.

Steven: You didn't know all those things?

Dr. June: No. Well, then another question we have is about the LGBT, okay? Because right now they're partnering with the LGBT. So how if they're saying that you're going to have the high morals, then how can you with sexual issues? How can they be back in and partnering with the LGBT agenda right now?

Jana: This is my personal because I understand what you're saying. Because the Noahide laws are against homosexuality. They are. They are. They're against homosexual ones.

Dr. June: Okay.

Jana: Right. No, they are. Right. Yeah. Yeah. So, under Noahide laws, homosexuals will be executed. Yeah. Here's the thing. As I told you in how they work, is they work through chaos.

Jana: Very bad. Okay. You can read it right there. You know, Sabbateans is out of the branch of the responsible for ruining morals of the Gentiles. They are the ones who introduced all these LGBT movement. They're the ones financing it, and the Noahide laws are going to fix that.

Dr. June: Wow. But they're the ones actually instigating it.

Jana: Well, you know. Do you know what Hegelian dialectic is? Yes. Okay. **They're going to create their own problems so they can have a solution.**

Steven: Let me speak on this issue here really quick, though, because one thing that a lot of people are not aware of, and I actually was just talking to a friend of mine in Israel about this very issue there. And they don't have to worry about beheading them in Israel, even though they've made this covenant. If you'll notice, where they have placed or where the majority of the homosexual community lives in Israel, it's on the coastline, Tel Aviv, etc. Right. Haifa, places like that. Well, as it was stated to me, quote unquote, "soon when the war begins, we will get rid of the riff raff."

Jana: Yeah.

Steven: All right. They have allowed them in that position. They're the secular Jews of Israel. And when and there also there is a major campaign going on right now that is not being publicized where they are going to the Jewish Orthodox Jewish communities in Europe. They're talking to them in America, but not as much as Europe to come home. And even if as quote unquote, as I was told, even if you have to live in a tent in Judea and Samaria, which is the West Bank, you come home. Now, why didn't they say live in a tent down there, you know, Tel Aviv or someplace like that? There's plenty of farmland. They could live in a tent down there.

Steven: They know that that's going to be bombed. They know that they're going to lose a mass loss of life. But what does what purpose do it serve, though? And Zohar prophecy and even biblical prophecy. But its prophecy has already been fulfilled. They talk about a third of the Jews have to die, right? Or two thirds will have to die. Right. So, they interpret that as being a third of the Jews in Israel, a third of the Jews in America. But see, they don't really care about them, and they want to select which third is killed. So therefore, they consider the homosexual community and secular Jews, they say, okay, wipe them out.

Steven: So, they put them in the harm's way so that when Iran does launch a bomb towards Israel, which biological and I was even told, quote unquote, from people in the intelligence community, they are fearful that Iran will use nuclear weapons. Well, I thought Iran didn't have nuclear weapons. Oh, yes, they do have nuclear weapons. And it was I forget I can't think of his name right now.

Steven: It's kind of slips my mind. But there is a friend of mine that interviewed an Iranian nuclear scientist, and that was is Jason. And yes, forgive me, brother. You know I love you. And, you know, I would remember, but that's my old age. And I got that part timers. So, part time I remember it anymore. So, but anyway, he interviewed the Iranian scientists and he told them, he said they already have three atomic bombs in Iran, and that was years ago. So, when Netanyahu is saying, well, we got to go to war with Iran because they have because they might get nuclear weapons, now they're getting more advanced.

Steven: And I know also directly why I can't say why I know it. I'll just say, yeah, yeah, China is funding Iran. **China is working closely with Iran, but China is also very close to Israel, major ally, and they are going to be the next world superpower.**

Jana: Is there an underground Sanhedrin?

Steven: Of course. The San. I mean that. What's that brother's name? That over there. Yes, they did build the Sanhedrin and I did ask that question from someone very high up in government about the fact that the Sanhedrin is going to replace or there is a desire in Israel that the

Sanhedrin will actually replace United Nations.

It is the desire of Israel that that will happen. And yes, that is what the goal is.

Brock: Yes. How do you think Trump will roll out the Noahide Laws? Do you think there will be a massive false flag where the UN openly takes over? Constitution suspended; the church is closed. Then the Noahide Laws?

Steven: No. That's probably the best one for you. Good job. You know, I will answer this part of it.

Jana: I just look at what he's supporting the entire process to peace and safety. Yeah, the entire process to peace and safety. And then having Jared Kushner there as advisor. This is all practice. **When you say the word Chabad think Noahide Laws.** This is what they are about. They are the proselytize for Noahide laws. This is their belief. Their basic theological belief is that Messiah is going to force Noahide laws on the nations you go to Chabad.org/Noahide laws. It's everywhere. It's there. They tell you that this is an incumbent upon all humanity. **All Gentile nations must accept Noahide laws. So is Trump.** How is he going to roll it out? He's already rolling it out by cooperation with the cabal the Trump needs to do is get away from Chabad Organization, get Jared Kushner out, start doing America first for real. Let's stop aid to Israel. We signed during lockdowns $38 billion in secrecy. The bill had no name. Do you understand? So, the thing is, we are here suffering as Americans. We lost jobs. We have depressions out of from lockdowns and poverty that is going on right now and taking away our rights. Trump needs to give us our rights back. Trump needs to get rid of Fauci.

Jana: Trump needs to **get away from Jared Kushner**. Trump needs to stop signing Noahide laws and get them out of public law immediately. So basically, until he does all of this and then also, he needs to give us truth on 9/11 and exactly what happened there. And he needs to immediately release us liberty documentary immediately in all four parts. That just was done by True News. They did.

Jana: We know the man who actually worked on this documentary, and you all need to know we have been attacked as a nation by Israel and it has been all whites. Yes. So, you need to understand that until Trump comes out with the whole nothing but the truth, we cannot vote for him.

Dr. June: I'd like to allude to this, if you don't mind. Yeah. Brock was watching the UN whenever they were talking about this one world peace. Now, can you explain to everybody what you, I believe, has to do with the Noahide Laws as well?

Brock: Well, they were all on script. So, you had Putin and Trump being they all hitting on some main points. One is, is that this is how the UN started in the past. They all gave a foundation of it. They went back and said, we started in the World War and then all these wars and then we met and this time in the Geneva. But now we're facing new things and we need to organize and come together for a new order. Was the gist of what I heard now. I was obviously wanting to hear what they'd be saying about it, and I heard that. I'm sure they were saying a lot of other stuff, but that's what I heard for sure. Now, with all of the rollout of COVID and all of the infrastructure money around the world, we're all going together. Right. And the incremental stages. You got stages of taking a little bit of the freedoms. And then one thing at a time being placed under Trump's authority or, hey, he's over infrastructure now. He's over, you know, let's see, agriculture. He was over, you know, the FTC communications, he was over this.

Now he put Jared Kushner over a lot of these supply chain.

Dr. June: For the vaccine implementation.

Brock: And everybody does. And he's systematically put him over the supply chain, over the Federal Trade Commission, over F.C.C., which is communications. There's our news and everything. So, with that being said, this is more of a question for me that I had. I saw the UN talking about a new order. If you go to a World Economic Forum, you see them talking about a Great Reset. Right? They talk about all of their agenda things, which are things right now the whole world agrees on hitting systematic racism, the LGBT inclusiveness.

Dr. June: At the mall yesterday with Jonathan Cahn, he talked about that, the systematic racism. He talked about Black Lives Matter.

Brock: They went down a UN agenda at our Christian gathering. Okay. So, with all of that being put under quote unquote, Trump state of emergency all around, right under Kushner. Every one of those. Where does that? I'd like to know where that falls in line with. I guess if there's a Noahide I mean, I could only imagine. But with that being said, what comes to y'all's mind? I'm just curious how that must line up with any kind of plan that you've heard or.

Dr. June: Question with the Chabad with Cohen, how he works in the UN all the time that's always pushing the Noahide agenda, you know, and then what Brock said that is them pulling that together, everybody giving it. What they do is they change the terminology. They don't come out and just say, we're implementing Noahide laws.

Steven: There's been too much said on Noahide laws now. And Jana really stirred that up with the world that has caused so many problems. They can't use that terminology.

Jana: Listen, before we started talking on Noahide laws, there were people talking about it, right? They were some individuals. Information was quite widely available online. We were talking about this on conferences and our chats and because of our platform, it got really out. What happened after is that all the algorithms changed in YouTube and everywhere I changed. Now, when you go research, Noahide laws, it's going to be difficult. Why you can't find it. I was just preparing this thing yesterday. It was like, where is all the stuff?

Jana: I had to search and search, and I had to go through DuckDuckGo, and I had to try. I mean, they are deleting it away now. Before we started talking about this, Israel 365 have wildly, wildly talked about Noahide laws all the time every other day. Wow. Now they don't even mention it all because you know, you can't know too much. Go in. You too smart. You too figured it out, you understand? So, they are changing terminology.

Steven: While they're on a rapid pace.

Dr. June: Jonathan Khan - it was me because I was friends with one of their board members about The Return. Me and Brock was talking about this on the way back. I talked to them in March about she was like, What? What's your objections against this? I should have never answered it because I just did a show where I expose like, oh, this is nothing about ecumenism I did, which is good. I've got it all still documented, but because of that **they changed the entire website and they made sure when they stood up there, they kept saying in the name of Jesus in the name, because I could tell you will not hear in the name of Jesus.** So, I know what you're saying about how they change them.

Steven: All right. Now, something that you guys need to know, and you need to really pay very close attention in the near future. A meeting I was in, and I can't say who or anything like that right now is in a meeting this weekend. And I have been told that there are major news events coming out very soon that is going to affect the Christian believers on a global scale. And we are working on I'll be working with a couple of other journalists to help you to know what those changes are when they're doing them and how it's going to affect us. But, you know, there are a lot of people in different positions that know about these things. They know it's coming. And so, we're going to really be working on this to let you know what's happening at this point. I don't know what those issues are. I've just been told that it's coming, major changes.

Steven: And after what you guys just discovered, are you and Brock from being there in DC and knowing this agenda and how clever they were to water it down to where it's interesting. The terminology was so patriotic that the Patriots had truly have truly sucked it right in thinking that they're talking about the founding fathers of America. Glory to God. We are. No, and it's not. So, let's go to the next question.

Dr. June: Okay, Dianna what is your next question?

Dianna: They are asking if the Illuminati and the Masons are part of the Noahide laws, and have they infiltrated the churches?

Steven: Oh, absolutely. They've infiltrated the churches. And yes, Freemasonry. **The 21st degree Mason is called the Noahide Mason.** I did a video on this a little while back when I was doing the research on this. From my perspective, Jana had done so much herself and I had discovered that the Orthodox Jews had infiltrated the Masons. And I'm not saying that the Masons were a good organization to begin with, but in the early years you had mainly just Christians that were in the Masons. Well, they did that in England and they were the ones that rewrote the laws for the Masons. **And when they did, they put the 21st degree Mason in there as a Noahide and he is the judge and executioner of the moral laws.** And I think that's also where the terminology moral law comes from. And of course, these are Zohar. Zohar clause. So, you ready to respond to that? Oh, and by the way, the 21st degree Mason look it up.

Steven: It's very interesting his because all the different degrees have different dress different ways that they do this, and you got to keep in mind to not you might know a lot of masons out there that probably have no clue to the inner workings. A lot of these guys that are masons, they just think, okay, we're taking the kids to the doctor and stuff and they're trying to do a good deed. These guys, I don't hold that against them. They really mean well with what they're trying to do. You know, they don't know that inner working in the in-depth part that's going on. So, they may even be somewhat high up, but they just don't know. **But that 21st degree Mason his dress is total black, black hood on with a sword.** So, he is the capital punishment judge of the Masons. So, I don't know how that's going to work out if it's just symbolic or will they actually carry out these laws.

Jana: Also, are you familiar with the Gray State trailer? Gray State?

Steven: Gray State.

Jana: Well, now I. Yeah, my color gray. Yeah, I, I don't remember the name. Maybe people who are watching can help me out. The name of a director who was making you forgot to I. Yeah, well, they killed him, and they killed his wife and. And the child, I think. Or two kids, I don't remember, because he had an inside information of what they're planning for this nation. And in that trailer, you could see and Noahide the mason freemason executing, decapitating people. And of course, no food, right?

Jana: The food production stopped and there was a revolution or civil war. And he wanted people to know.

Brock: David and his wife and his child are found dead?

Jana: Yes. Yes. And his movie could never come to fruition.

Brock: It's the same thing I'll talk about. All right. So, we know biblically that you have Satan, and he has a hierarchy of principalities, powers and dominions and names and everything. Right. Inner workings, just like a military country. Everything territories in this satanic. I'd like to see if we could do some clarity for people, because right now you have like a medusa and many heads of those snakes and a bunch of heads coming. Satan is the art of war. Been here doing the art or Sun Tzu? He's been doing this since the beginning of time. He has the Cabal, right? And you have all these different heads of the Brotherhood you got, you know, Illuminati and all these different organizations, right? Masons. And he goes down everything.

Brock: Any idea on Satan's never going to make it so that it's playing this person, this organization is over. This one, they're all working, and they all think they're the ones working directly with Satan. They're all his special ones, but all of those veins flow down from there. And if you had any idea on clarity on how that works?

Dr. June: Like the hierarchy. The Catholics, Jews.

Brock: From what I understand, is some of them focus on different things. Cabal does work with a lot of the money side and the power, for example, the Rockefellers, Rothschilds, all of them guys, they we purchased the state of Israel. They have a little puppet like it goes down and Soros does this and then work and he has the Illuminati, right? Illuminati does their things with the arts, with music and things like that. You got brotherhood who work there. They're a witch organization that specifically tear down churches. They work in all the hospitals in our country to kill people. When you go to the hospital, they you'll have disorders, what you call the brotherhood. They basically, you know, in hospitals, they feed on killing and hurting. And people like when you come in and you got a thing and people say, I don't know why, I just turn for the worse. I don't know why I can't figure out why they just can't find it in me. These spirits have infirmities, they curse. And the more they kill, they get powerful and stronger demons. And these witches have their headquarters in LA, right there feeding. It's just like all of this stuff are inter behind the scenes working. And it's not conspiracy. This stuff is real.

Brock: The books out there you can read on this, people who are in it, who got saved and delivered. Right. And free. I just wanted to kind of, I guess, clarify, and let people know there are inner organizations. Satan has a lot of things organized out there who affect the different flows of all of the world system. And if the church would just get themselves organized and treat it legitimately an organization territory, one person at a time that you freed from his kingdom, that this is what it's going to boil down to us, doing what we're told to do. And it is taking one person at a time from those I mean thoughts on this.

Steven: I think Brock laid it out pretty good already.

Brock: That's all I know now.

Steven: Right? Right. I just you know it.

Dr. June: All right. Well, let's move forward with the Noahide laws with Dianna. Do you have one?

Dianna: Yeah, several people are asking when like the time frame of when they'll actually be implemented and actually upheld.

Jana: So, I can give you something I think only because when you study Chabad.org/Noahide laws, they say that Moshi, he's going to enforce Noahide laws upon the nations.

Jana: So, they're preparing the infrastructure, they are preparing the laws, they're preparing everything. And when they, you know, they have to Moshi's anyway, they have just perfect messiah, as I explain to you. So, whoever it is, they will say he will enforce Noahide laws upon the nations. That's what they believe. They also believe that Davidic Messiah and the Davidic Messiah nations were the only ones left, will be the only of the nations who willingly do Noahide laws.

This is all Chabad.org, so I only say it from their point of view, but when they get to do it, will they be successful fully? You know, as Brock says, we the church, we have the power, but we don't use it. We don't really realize it because we are handy. Well, I'm not saying we here, but church is handing the power over to the beast.

Jana: We are whether it is whether this is done willingly or unknowingly, but I think it's mostly unknowingly because they are not properly educated on Judaism. So that's what.

MY THOUGHTS:

It's so amazing to go back and read this two years later. It is more relevant today than it was back then. Wow!

END-TIMES WATCHMAN CONFERENCE 2020 W/STEVE & JANA BEN-NUN, PAMELA SHUFFERT, JEFF BYERLY, CELESTE SOLUM, & DR. JUNE KNIGHT. HOSTS ARE BROCK & LAURA KNIGHT

(*Most viewed conference on the internet* – May 2020)

Brock: Here we go. Okay, everyone, we are live. All right. I'm going to go ahead and mute that on my end. Okay. Well, everyone, we are extremely excited here today. We have a lineup that is extremely powerful. And my name is Brock Knight, and this is my lovely wife, Laura.

Brock: Each of these people here have respective fields where they have had a lot of experience or God has been speaking to them or, one or the other, they have had things happen to them and they have become awake. And we are hoping to summarize what you guys need to hear and see that what's going on right now in the world around you. It is happening. I'd like to ask each of these people one question, and that is this: What do these people need to know from what you're seeing and what you're experiencing, what is going on right now that they need to be awake and aware? Maybe the top three things that we need to know from yours and if we can start with you, Miss Celeste, that would be amazing.

If you could share with us, what do we need to know from what you're seeing?

Celeste: Okay, so I just posted just before we came on about the Mark of the Beast and the link between the hydrogel and the quantum dots and the masks. And I will tell you, the stuff that I got coming out about and it fits in with Deuteronomy 32 in Revelation 13 is explosive. So, we need to be serious students of history, biblical history and just the other holocausts in history so that we can be prepared.

Brock: Thank you. Thank you. I'd like to go to Israeli News right now.

Steve: It is the most serious bringing about of a one world Religion. We know we have a one world government or New World Order; however, people want to call that, and in the Pentagon, they tell me they call it a one world government there. But the one world religion aspect is the most serious because what's happening today is there there has been a major infiltration inside of Christianity in every walk that there is. They don't care whether you're Pentecostal, Catholic, Methodist, even non-denomination. **There has been an infiltration of Talmudic Rabbis that have infiltrated even in Catholicism, to bring the children of God back underneath Talmudic Rabbis of today.** And when I first began to expose the early stages, I did not realize that they were trying to bring us up underneath the Rabbis. I thought that they were trying to bring all the churches underneath the Catholic Church, which they were doing. And then at the same time that the Catholic Church was forming the alliance called the Nostra Aetate with Israel, I began to really blast this about eight years ago, Laurie Cardoza-Moore really came down heavy on me over this.

She was a friend of ours and so she flew to our house in Florida here and had a private meeting with me and she said, "You've got to keep your mouth shut about these issues here because we've been working on this for years".

Steve: I didn't know how deep this really went though, and as time went on, I really discovered the ultimate part of this. Yes, the Catholic Church was working to bring all the denominations together under them, but the Pope of Rome would then submit his authority completely over to the Rabbinic rabbis and this is where the problem is coming in, which has also caused me to go back and really examine Biblical scriptures because I do understand the Hebrew language as well, so I look at that and I'm seeing a lot of prophecies that we have futurized actually were fulfilled by Christ or fulfilled by the Apostles, things of this nature here and I see that we're about to put Jesus Christ to an open shame once again and crucify Him afresh by this very thing.

Jana: And then also this new government that has now the coalition formed by Bibi Netanyahu and Gantz is kind of worrisome. We are getting word from the Jews in Israel who believe in Christ, who accepted Jesus as Messiah, that they are going to be under tremendous persecution because the Orthodox rabbis are gaining power in a state of Israel. And of course, in 2014, in the year of 2014, Benjamin Netanyahu promised rabbis that he's going to make Israel a Talmudic state, that Israel will be and the under legal code of Talmud.

And we know that officially in Talmud, Christians are not well spoken of, and Jesus is not well spoken of as well. And they do not want to tolerate Christianity, or especially Jews who believe in Jesus in Israel. So, they're persecuting them, even though it's not really official. If you Google it, you can find some articles about it, but we did interview several Christians from the state of Israel who admitted that they are being persecuted. They are being ... Their passports are being taken away from them. They are under threat of even losing their (religion), their citizenship, because if they made Aliyah as Jews to Israel, but they converted to Christianity or accepting Jesus as the Messiah; under Talmud they're not considered Jews anymore, so they are threatening them to throw them out of the state of Israel. If a Jew is married to a non-Jew Gentile ... we had a specific case ...

Steve: Actually, we've had more than one case - several cases that we know of personally in Israel - but one good friend of mine there, his wife was put in prison. They threatened her and she had to leave her husband because he was born Jewish, even though he's a believer, and they fought it and finally they threw his wife out of the country.

Jana: Yes, and they kept her in prison with only like one slice of bread a day and they wouldn't provide any hygienic, er, no toothbrush, no comb for the hair. It was like a torture, basically, until they threw her out of the country. So, he found himself without a wife. And these kinds of things are going on inside of the state of Israel and the Christians in Israel are very worried, especially Jewish Christians, are very worried of this coalition of guns and Bibi Netanyahu, because they are giving too much power to the religious right, which is Orthodox Judaism - the rabbis.

Brock: Right. And Miss Pam, you had shared some knowledge on this. Would you like to further on that same topic and help us out with what you're seeing, please?

Pam: Well, yes, I would. And thank you so much, Steve and Jana, to build on that. I, for years, was involved in outreach to Jewish communities; Russian Jews in Chicago and New York City, and spent much time with messianic Jews, studied some Hebrew, lived in Jerusalem a while. And, you know, as I got involved in my investigative journalism of 25 years ago, I began to put together pieces to my years of being in the Jewish communities in Brooklyn, New York, where Lubavitch, Chabad is, and many others who are feverishly working towards getting a new messiah and definitely bringing forth a new world order, which is really, in fact, for many Jews out there - not all. I will not stereotype to seek to bring persecution against the Jews, that is despicable - but for many Jews, the New World Order is really a Jew world order, their Jewish world government that they seek to set up from Jerusalem taking various scriptures, and I've spent time among those Jews in Brooklyn, New York, and that is why they have the Noahide laws to get rid of millions of Gentiles who will not renounce their faith in Jesus because they believe that Jesus, according to the Talmud, was a terrible sinner, the product of a harlot and a Roman soldier. The Talmud teaches this and says Christians should be killed. They believe there's no place for Christians who dare to confess Jesus is the Son of God and divine. And therefore, I began to put all of this together as, years later in my journalism, what I learned living in Jewish communities, living in Jerusalem a while, and getting straight from people directly, learning many, many things. But I will say, yes, absolutely. I have hard core evidence that churches have been infiltrated by people of the Satanic Globalist New World Order agenda, and I got it straight from the horse's mouth, former CIA. And by the way, the CIA is one of the most satanic antichrist, kill the Christians New World Order Agency in the World Today, a direct product of Nazis meeting at the Wannsee Conference to decide that if the New World Order failed under Nazi Germany and the agenda - and Hitler was a Satanist of the Illuminati - they would transport the whole agenda to America and thus was born the CIA. Ever since they've come to America, they have worked feverishly nonstop in every wicked capacity they can to bring America down, down, down, under the New World Order and they have infiltrated the churches. You've got the Jewish elements of the New World Order working feverishly to infiltrate Christian religious organizations and the Vatican. Then you have the Gentile side with these Nazis and their imports from Germany to Operation Paperclip, bringing thousands of German Nazis, SS Gestapo through into America, through Operation Paperclip to continue the Nazi, very fascist Nazi Satanic Antichrist agenda from the Gentile side for the New World Order agenda.

Pamela: And this one man, a 30-year vet and the CIA admitted he said, "Oh, there's not one Christian institution or church or Bible college we have not infiltrated to a greater or lesser degree". And I found out the CIA, through my many ex-CIA, now Christians, who came out to blow the whistle, they told me they've got a computer. **The CIA developed a computer to spy on every church across America.** They have the names of every member, every pastor, and **even rating Christians according to well, are they fake?** Are they lukewarm? Are they serious Christians? We are being spied upon by the intelligence community. And furthermore, they were planting their groomed spy agents, just like the KGB spied on churches in Russia - and I also speak Russian (speaks in Russian) - I have spent years with Russian Christians in America and among Russian Jews and I found out horror stories of the KGB spies of Russia, the Communist spies infiltrating the churches as pastors and priests and Christians don't know it today. They have been deceived and hoodwinked. But the same thing is happening in America today, including in Pentecostal churches, Baptist churches. **You would be shocked to know how many are actually Jesuits, the Vatican, Masons, Satanists or CIA groomed spies to monitor the faithful and eventually to lead them out under the guise of Romans 13, you must obey the government.**

Pamela: Out to FEMA camps, boxcars and shackles, to be killed as resisters of the New World Order agenda. And my CIA sources coming out after many years of working for the New World Order

Agenda said, "We all know what the FEMA camps are for in America. **We know they are to terminate the future resisters of the New World Order as it comes down in America under martial law.** And one source said, "Yes, we hated the Christians so much because they stand in the way in America of our New World Order agenda". She said it will be - and I'm sorry to quote this, but I must wake up the church because it's far more serious than you think - she said that under martial law, **when they start arresting all these millions of people and Christians on the New World Order hit list, it will be brutal rape, torture and death for the Christians that they hate so much in the CIA.** These FEMA camps are death camps. They are not quarantine camps, medical camps. **These are termination camps, much as Hitler's concentration camps and the horrors of the Holocaust or the Bolshevik Communists or the horrors of the gulags.** We have the same thing set up today and this is a time for the church across America to get educated, wake up and realize the date and hour we live in and the dangers we face now. This is the most important thing I can tell them.

Pamela: Church wake up and, furthermore, quit playing church. If you're living for Jesus on Sunday and then living for the devil the rest of the week, you're not going to make it. You'd better repent and get right with God. Now there is far too much compromise in the Churches of America today, and I know this from living on the grounds of a former, prosperous, well known Christian television ministry, which finally fell because of sin and is no more. But when I was there working there 30 years, I saw a cross section working in that ministry with people coming from all over the world, all over America, of the churches in America today. And I could not believe the level of sin, compromise, cyber porn, adultery, fornication, and the sin that crept into the ministry itself, which is why it fell. It broke my heart and the heart of God. I said, "Lord, these people, they're not going to have the grace they need to stand against great persecution, including Revelations 20v4: the souls of them beheaded for the witness of Jesus. I've been documenting my military, Pentagon, military family background. My father was in the Pentagon, I was born in the headquarters of US Air Force. I have many contacts out there. **Yes, the rumors you've been hearing about guillotines in America are 100% correct and not urban legend.** They tie in with Bible prophecy. Revelation.

Brock: Pam, let me hold you right there, because people listening right now are like, okay, we just heard about something from Celeste and like, whoa, we just heard things from Steve and Jana, like ... are you serious? They're doing that to Jews? And there's a one world religion? Okay. Whoa. Okay. And then you're saying CIA, is of the devil and this stuff is happening now. These people may not ... they're like, okay, wouldn't Trump be ridding all the evil force? Now, Mom, June Knight - you've been at the White House as a correspondent. These people are thinking, okay, is this conspiracy theory? Am I looking at people who know the Lord or are they just out there? Now, here's what we want to do. Mom, you've been looking at executive orders every day and you literally go live. You read everything that's going on in the government executive orders. You even take the time to read it in front of people for them to see if there's ... people don't want to hear this, do they? We share this but people, they just block. So, Mom, what would you share that you were seeing from the White House and the ecumenical movement or the apostasy, this church movement that's moving towards this one world religion and the government? What would you say to that?

Dr. June: All of this affects the entire globe. So, what I'm telling you is, I'm very sorry to have to report to a lot of you that believe the narrative that you see on the mainstream media where Trump is the savior. You know, he's the one, he's the only one that defends patriotism and he's the only one who loves the country. You know what I mean? I'm very sorry to tell you that it is all propaganda. And it was hard for me to find out that it was propaganda, but. I'm telling you tonight that it is propaganda. So, the top three things that I want you to know is this. Okay, first of all, **President (Trump) is with the UN.** Listen to me. He is globalist. Okay? So, you need to understand, because a lot of people out there do not believe he's globalist because of the narrative that's being said on TV. But he is globalist. He is working with the UN. He is putting in the infrastructure across the entire globe, not just the United States, but the entire globe of 5G, which is the power to the Beast, the A.I. that is being set up now. Okay? It is going to bring such control over all of us. We have not seen anything until they click that power switch.

Dr. June: I want you to know, number one, the President is not what he portrays himself to be. I was, I felt like I was his number one fan. I did two national Christian marches for him, not for him, but, you know, believing in him. The last one was the Trump 2020 campaign. I did that in front of the White House - the *Evangelicals for Trump*. I'm the one who coined that, by the way, *Evangelicals for Trump*, Trump 2020. But I had to do it even though I already found out that he was not for us because I already had it planned. I made sure when I went to that march that I obeyed the Lord and read the speech that God gave to me in a dream, warning the President one last time, him and the Republicans, **if you do not turn from this perversion, judgment is going to hit this nation so fast.** Well, they made their decision and now we're going, we're headed straight into this tsunami. So, the first thing that I want you to know is that **he is with the UN; he is globalist.** And I'm very sad. It took me six months of grieving to get over how sad I was. Okay, number two, he is partnering with the vaccine implementation. There is a big misunderstanding out there that he is not for the vaccine implementations. They say, "Oh, Trump said we don't have to have the vaccine". Well, let me tell you something. He very much believes that you do. **So just hear me good, because he assigned a czar, a vaccine czar. So, if he was not serious about his agreement with the U.N., he would not get a czar, which is their full, their full mission is to make sure that this agenda is fulfilled.** Then before he got the czar, about three weeks prior, he formed he called in a million-man army. Listen to me. When he first called in that Million Man Army,

Dr. June: I'm like, what do we need with a Million Man Army? This was back when they were telling everybody, "Oh, this is only temporary. You only need to wear your mask temporary. You only need to do your six-foot distancing. Just temporary right now" and then he forms this million-man army, then a few weeks later, he appoints his czar. He has broken - the third thing I want to tell you - is that he has broken the country up into four quarters.

Dr. June: Listen to me.

1. **In 2020, the first quarter was the rollout of the vaccine** where they said this is the problem. They did the press conferences every day in the White House. I was with him every day. I had my team with me, and we watched it and we examined everything he said. I read all the executive orders to everybody, etc., etc. So, after the first quarter where he scared everybody to death with this huge virus that he's saying is happening. He presented the problem. **He formed his million-man army in that first quarter.** So, you're thinking, why are you doing this?

2. **The second quarter, he rolls out the testing.** He rolls out the testing in the second quarter where he says he wants everyone tested. So, what he did is he put it all in his name. **Everything has to be in his name.** He put it in his name and said, all of you governors, you have to fulfill this mandate before you can open up. This is why you see a lot of the governors out there going crazy, trying to get it done so fast. That's why they're

clamping down on people in there so hard is because the president yes, your president has put the clamp on them and said you either do this or else. That's the second quarter, it's the testing.

3. **The third quarter he calls the transition to greatness.** I'm thinking, what is the transition to greatness? Okay, let's tell you what it is.

  a. First quarter: January, February, March - identify the problem.

  b. Second quarter: April, May, June - we're finishing that quarter. Lawlessness broke out by his will under his watch. Lawlessness is breaking out for a reason.

  c. Now we're getting ready to step into the third quarter, which is July. What's happening in July? The peace deal they're saying is going to be finalized in July. **They're going to split the land in Israel.** Then we're stepping into September. In September, you're going to have all of the new world order heads in Washington, D.C., including the apostasy you are going to have all the apostasy, the New Apostolic Reformation leaders are going to be in Washington for Jonathan Cahn's event called The Return with the rabbis, which goes along with this Noahide Laws agenda that they have. They have all of them there in September. Then you're going to have the G-7. The president - by the way, your president is the president of G-7, which is the top seven global countries, which is underneath the UN. So, all of you that think he's not globalist, you are sorely missing it. The G-7 has been moved. It was supposed to be on June the 12th in the White House and they moved it to September. Wonder why? Wonder why they're going to have the top seven leaders of the world, the heads of the U.N. in Washington, D.C., in September at the same time that they are going to have the apostasy leaders, the new world religion leaders there, then you're going to have the new world economy leaders there and then you're going to have the new world government leaders there. The economy. They are getting ready for a global vaccine conference all at the same time. **All the heads of New World Order are going to be in Washington, D.C. in September. That is the final month of transition to greatness that the president is calling for.**

d. **Then you go into the fourth quarter, which is the vaccine rollout.** The fourth quarter is the part where they're going to finish their plan, their final plan in September, and then they're going to implement it in the fourth quarter and the president has said about **2021 5G will be implemented.** All devices will be antiquated by then and it's going to be a new world. **I'm just telling you all that your president is not the way that he portrays himself and he is globalist.**

Brock: So that leads me in to asking Celeste. We have this vaccine that we all know is coming. It's very clear when our government doesn't talk about building your immune system. And all they talk about from the very beginning isn't the vaccine. The vaccine. The vaccine. What would you say to people in terms of vaccine and the mark of the beast or any type of surveillance of nanotechnology and vaccines? People want to know, is it conspiracy theories? As a Christian, should we be even thinking and talking like this? What would you say?

Celeste: So, it's absolutely real. It is not any ordinary vaccine. **There are nanoparticles in it.** Whether you believe it's the hydrogen or the quantum dots. When it gets into your body, it assembles and it grows and it fuses to all your cells, all your muscles, all your bones. **So, if you change your mind later down the road, it's not possible.** It's not like an RFID that you can dig out because it becomes one with you. But that's not the most horrifying thing. **The most horrifying thing is you become one with artificial intelligence.** You become your own computer interface. You don't need your laptop anymore. You don't need your computer. You don't need to carry credit cards anymore. **You are part of the hive.** And what I discovered in this breaking news that I just did is that it **changes your DNA**. *It basically you are blotted out from being a human to the degree that Jesus does not recognize you.* So, this is in the vaccine, just even if that wasn't enough, there are **there's the quantum and hydrogen element.** There are humanized mice.

Celeste: These are mice that have human immune systems, organs, blood, the whole ten yards, aborted babies, humanized plants. Those are plants where they took humans and mix them contrary to scripture, where it says do not mix species.

Celeste: You know, in the very beginning of the Bible and we know what happened in Genesis 6. Plus, it's got sterilization chemicals and some other chemicals in it too. It is extremely dangerous. They're going to put it in a blender and say, voila, you know, this is going to protect you from a pathogen. **And I'm here to tell you that if you inject this devil's concoction that includes hydrogen and quantum dots and aborted babies and humanized mice and humanized plants and all these chemicals, you're setting yourself up for destruction.** It's not going to protect you. *God will not honor your health.*

Brock: Okay, so here we are. We're in, this panel says we're in the last days.

Pam: Yes, sir.

Brock: A mark of the beast or some beast, a system that's being held. And then next year, Trump says beginning of the year, we have 5G released all over the world. So, we have the capabilities with the supercomputers, with all the 5G capabilities or a digital intranet out there that covers the grid. Okay.

Brock: Next, we have the topic of the church with mom. You have mentioned the apostasy. These people are wondering apostasy. Whoa. Okay. Now it says in the Bible that even the elect will be deceived, that people who truly believe they walk with the Lord and most certainly more than likely do. But they're on a road or a path and they're being deceived. Mom, what would you say? And you mentioned the NAR or the New Apostolic Reformation. What would you say that gives proof in all your travel and meeting and working with these leaders?

Dr. June: It's perversion. This is what turned me away from the president is when I saw the partnership with the evangelicals, him and perversion.

Brock: Evangelicals. What do you mean? Like who? What are you talking about? You don't have to say names. We don't want to. But what do you mean? The evangelicals?

Dr. June: What I mean is the body of Christ has been so happy that we have had representation in the **White House with Paula White being in there, which, by the way, she is over an ecumenical team.** It's not evangelicals. They are all religions that she's over. She is ecumenical. And just to let you know what ecumenical is, ecumenical is when you blend with all religions, you dumb Jesus down and you partner with and make all the gods the same.

Dr. June: And that is what they're trying to do with this one world religion is they're trying to make everything the same. Like in the State Department, they have a division, a project called the *Abrahamic Faiths Initiative*, which me and Miss Jana and Steve, were talking about this last night. The *Abrahamic Faith Initiative* is taking the top three religions. You have the Jews, the Christians, which, by the way, are evangelicals who sold us out and put us under the Catholic Church. Okay, so now, when they say Christians, they put us under Catholics. So, you take the Christians, the Jews and the Muslims and they are trying to put them together under this program called the Abrahamic Faiths Initiative, where they make everybody the same God, except if you call your God, Jesus. This is where the problem comes in, because Jesus is offensive, because we say - the Christians - that he is the only way to heaven. And this is where, this is where the issue comes in, Brock.

Brock: Okay. So, Pam, now I'm sitting here and I'm a listener. I've never heard any of you before. I've never heard any of this. And I'm sitting here like I don't even ... I'm turning this off, I can't handle this. Here's what I'd ask you. Where's proof? What do I look up? What can I find out? Where is it out? Because do they not do this stuff in plain sight? Isn't it there for me to find? If it is, tell me where to find proof.

Pam: Now you're asking me then, Brock, ,about proof of what the guillotines, Noahide laws or guillotines or FEMA camps or ...?

Brock: Let's just start one of these and I'm going to ask each of you if you can give proof, obviously, but let's talk about the church selling out, the pope. Where can I find proof that the Pope is out there promoting himself as a one religion that we all believe the same? Is there proof?

Pamela: There are articles out there coming out all the time. In fact, I read a great article by brother Nathaniel Kempner, a Jew who converted to Jesus. He put out a great article about the Pope accepts and embraces the Noahide Laws, which will lead to the massive worldwide genocide of Christians through the guillotines, Noahide Laws, Christians breaking two of them. The Pope embraced the Noahide Laws which spell genocide, and you can look this up online. Oh, yes, **the Vatican has a great love affair with these people, and they've accepted the Noahide Laws, which, unless you are willing to renounce your faith in Jesus as the son of God and divine, the Jews call that blasphemy and idolatry then you would deserve beheading.** Yes, I've studied this thoroughly and through working with Jews. I got an email once from a Jewish reader of my reports who said, Lady, your reporting is 100% correct. And the anti-Christ you, you Christian's fear will be our new messiah to lead us to world conquest and get rid of you. You Christians who stand in our way and they'll get rid of us by the Noahide Laws prophesied in Revelation 20, verse four. The souls of them beheaded for the witness of Jesus under a 666 Antichrist government. This is Bible prophecy, the end of the end times falling into place perfectly.

Pamela: And when you stand in front of a military soldier in full military uniform who says, Well, ma'am, it's all true. Yes, we have guillotines at Fort Lewis McChord, Washington, and I'm returning, when I returned from being off on leave, I'm going to train all 64 men in my platoon in how to operate the modern military guillotines we have in a top secret building partly underground there in Fort Lewis, Tacoma, Washington. Oh, I've spent 25 years documenting these things. I hate urban legends and wildfire rumors. I get right in the faces of former CIA military truck drivers who've been delivering the guillotines across America by truck eyewitnesses, truckers admitting it like one did in a church not long ago. The evidence is everywhere. The problem is **people don't want to hear these things because it's too painful for the human heart and mind and Christians to receive it.** Many will turn it off immediately. You give them all the proof you want, but they retreat quickly into their safety, comfort, denial zones. Because the truth is too painful for these people to grasp but they have to hear. They have to listen because they are the targets of the wrath of the Satanic Illuminati base, Satan space, new world order agenda. They're coming to destroy our faith.

Brock: I'm listening to this and I'm like, wow, I know it says in the Bible that they'll have itching ears. They want to hear what they want to hear. Right? Where can we go? And at the end of this, obviously, people will know how to find each of your information to do further research. And we highly recommend you to. Steve, what would you say in terms of proof? I mean, is this really happening? Is this stuff ...

Jana: Yes. I'm going to go first. I want to talk about some proofs, especially **when it comes to Noahide Laws because Christian communities, especially Christian leaders, are divided on that issue.** However, when you look at proofs, then it makes you think what Noahide Laws are and why they are important in terms of end times. I'm looking right now in my computer. I don't have a chance to share it here on the screen. I'm looking at the **official document that was signed in 2007, on March 11th between Catholic Church and Jewish rabbis, the highest degree, the very elite Jewish rabbis of Israel** and I'm looking at this; it's a commission for religious relations with the Jews. The Catholic Church has signed this document. The delegation of the Holy See Commission for Religious Relations with the Jews and the Chief Rabbinate of Israel Delegation for Relations with the Catholic Church. Now, they have several points in the document, and they are saying that <u>the **Pope has signed that the Jewish tradition emphasizes the Noahide Covenant as containing the universal moral code which is incumbent on all humanity.**</u>

Jana: So basically, they agreed the Noahide Covenant, which are <u>seven Noahide Laws, which are Talmudic, and they are specific in Talmud. They're not biblical, they're Talmudic, they're incumbent on all humanity.</u> Now I also have another document that's easily to be looked up, and I can provide you links, and you can provide this in your description. I<u>'m looking at United Nations document, they had united the United Nations with the seven Noahide Laws when all the diplomats, delegates and emissaries gathered at United Nations</u>

headquarters for *One People One World Conference*. **Well, they have all signed and agreed that Noahide Covenant is the covenant incumbent upon all humanity.**

Jana: The **chief rabbinate of Israel has made a relationship with the scholars of the Muslim world, with the Muslims, and they have agreed that the Sharia Law and the Noahide Law are basically synonymous.** *They're synonymous.*

Steve: Let me just throw something out there, Brock, as well. What's important for people to understand when we look at Noahide Laws is that **it is a capital punishment for violation of each of those laws**. They are Talmudic, they're not biblical, even though they try to make it biblical. I have the Encyclopedia Britannica of Talmud behind me here. That's what I call it, because it's not one book, it's about 25 books. But you mentioned proof. I want to give you some very strong proof here, one, As guillotines have been mentioned I spent, I would say, more like entry level, **seven years in the CIA**. I know politicians from presidents, governors, senators, etc., and I know how corrupt it is. This was from '83 to '91. **I also spent more than 25 years in the Chabad Lubavitch movement,** so I know just how corrupt that is as well. So, I know firsthand knowledge on these. I have a lot of colleagues and a lot of people, former colleagues from work I did. I know Intelligence people from all over the world, different countries, etc., and I stay in touch with a lot of these. I know the very man who works directly in the White House has been there since Ronald Reagan.

Steven: The man that ordered the guillotines brought into the United States in pieces because I was told that according to the Constitution, US Constitution, they could not order guillotines in. This was under the Obama administration, so they piecemealed it out; a half million guillotines. All right. I even know the number of how many was ordered. **Speaking of the Noahide Laws, the 21st degree Mason - when the Masonry was infiltrated back in the 1800s by Jewish people that came in and started writing these things - the 21st degree Mason is called the Noahide Mason, and his entire garb is that of an executioner.**

21. Noachite, or Prussian Knight Degree

The history, as well as the character, of this degree is a very singular one. It is totally unconnected with the series of degrees founded upon the Temple of Solomon, and is completely unrelated to the Temple of Zerubbabel or to other Masonic legends and traditions of later history. The history upon which the degree rests is traced to the Tower of Babel; hence the Prussian Knights called themselves Noachites, or Disciples of Noah, while they designate other Masons as Hiramites, or Disciples of Hiram.

The destruction of the Tower of Babel constitutes the legend of the Degree, whose mythical founder is said to have been Peleg, the chief builder of the edifice. A singular regulation is that there shall be no artificial light in the Lodge Room, and that the meetings shall be held on the night of the full moon of each month. The Degree, as is readily seen, is an unfitting link in Scottish Rite Masonry, an interruption in the chain of legendary symbolism, substituting Noah for Solomon, and Peleg for Hiram Abif. But it can not be denied that the Degree has distinctive Masonic value; it supports the more or less difficult proposition that the whole earth was peopled as a result of the dispersion at Babel, all peoples and nations descending from the three sons of Noah.

The legend describes the travels of Peleg from Babel to the North of Europe, and ends with the following narrative: "In trenching the rubbish of the saltmines of Prussia was found in A.D. 553, at a depth of fifteen cubits, the appearance of a triangular building in which was a column of white marble, on which was written in Hebrew the whole history of the Noachites. At the side of this column was a tomb of freestone on which was a piece of agate inscribed with the following epitaph: Here rests the ashes of Peleg, our Grand Architect of the Tower of Babel. The Almighty had pity on him because he became humble." The particular charge of this Degree is that Masons are to be modest and humble, not vainglorious and filled with self-conceit; that they are never to place themselves above Deity or claim greater wisdom than possessed by him; nor are they to find fault with his works, nor endeavor to improve

17

Jana: If you don't mind, I want to quickly mention that the **Noahide Covenant was passed as a part of the 2030 agenda in the United Nations in 2016.** Right before the, before the election of President Trump, they had the conference and they have proposed to the United Nations to pass it as a part exactly the part of 2030 agenda. It was passed, and on that particular conference, we have a video on our Patron channel where there was one Jewish rabbi who was very happy because he was saying that President Trump ...

Steve: Cohen

Jana: No, it wasn't. Cohen It was a different rabbi, the president, that he was kind of saying, **we are very happy because the future president is on with the Noahide agenda with us, and he agrees to it**. Now we know that in 1991, Noahide Laws were passed as a public law. It was passed into the United States law system as a public law, it's under education. Education Day. It's always on the Schneerson birthday. They are the ... Schneerson was the leader of a Chabad Hassidic group most influential leader and he's the one who started promoting seven Noahide Talmudic laws, and they started re-signing them in the White House every single year.

Jana: Now, some people think that these laws are only ceremonial, however, public laws are quite important. They are laws that are public. We talk a lot of ... yes, we consulted attorneys who basically said, No, that's part of our law and lets us not forget that it was the public law that got the United States into the United Nations. We were part as, part of the United Nations under public law. So, they do take those public laws quite seriously, especially when there is no more constitution. Now, Stephen mentioned Nostra Aetate when the **Catholic Church signed Nostra Aetate,**[9] which was the relations with the Jews back with the Jews, because until then, the Catholic Church was quite anti-Semitic. They were promoting a lot of things against Jews, and they decided that they're going to make relations now with the Jewish community and Jewish rabbis, especially the Judaism, Talmudism that is. And **Nostra Aetate document was drafted and later written and signed by Catholic bishops who were Jews.** They were Jewish rabbis who, for the purpose of signing Nostra Aetate, converted to Catholicism. They have drafted it, they have written it, passed it. And then after it was all done, they have converted back to Judaism.

Jana: It was actually done by the Jews. They infiltrated the Catholic Church. **The elite rabbis of Chabad organization or Chabad Hasidic Jews are very anti-Christian.** So again, **we have the seven Noahide laws are part of 2030 agenda,** as I have explained and it's going to be very important after 2030 world. So, they're preparing it at something after, I guess, when Messiah comes, and when you go to Chabad.org, it explains that Messiah will enforce seven Noahide Laws on all the Gentiles. Now again, seven Noahide Laws are incumbent

---

[9] https://www.npr.org/2015/11/01/453448972/nostra-aetate-opened-up-catholic-jewish-relations-50-years-ago

only on Gentiles, as we know ... **613 laws are for the Jews, seven for the Gentiles.**

Jana: And **under these laws, Gentiles can be executed by decapitation and then execution is mentioned in the Talmud.**

Pamela: That's right.

Jana: ... and it was also written on Cohen's website, who is a member of United Nations, he is basically a member there in United Nations - and it was on his website for public to see that it will be decapitation that will be done for any of the violations of seven Noahide Laws and under the first law which says no idolatry, **Christians who worship Jesus Christ are considered idolaters.**

Pamela: Amen. That's right.

Jana: So, they are going to be forced to denounce Jesus eventually,

Pamela: Correct.

Jana: You know, because those laws are part of Agenda 2030 now.

Jana: So, they are preparing it for whatever one world religion they're going to pass.

Brock: My goodness. Thank you so much. Now ... to my Mom. You were in the UN in New York, in the United Nations, filming.

June: Yes.

Brock: They were in there talking about the faith. I can't remember what they call that part, but it was the Agenda 2030, and they were on the topic of faith. You were looking down and you were seeing evangelicals that I grew up seeing on TBN.

June: Yes.

Brock: I mean, preachers that I've read books and listened to a lot of tapes and learned from about faith and about, I mean, you name it. Right? These ministers sitting down there, sitting beside LGBTIQ . Am I wrong? They were sitting beside the leaders of the LGBTIQ community, which, by the way, are trying to add F to their alphabet now for faith? Isn't that something?

June: Yes, it's terrible.

Pamela: Terrible

Brock: And then were they not sitting right beside the Noahide Law guy?

June: Yes, they were sitting beside the Noahide Laws guy, and he was sitting right in front of the president and what made me so sick is I was sitting next to TruNews. So, we were taking our cameras and we were zooming the crowd and closing in on the evangelicals because it's like, can you believe our evangelicals are in the UN. partnering with this UN agenda? And now what do we see? Well, they've already partnered with Kanye. I mean, they've already partnered with the cultural view. You see a lot of the people, a lot of the big Christian leaders now doing the Together campaign with the UN. So, yes, they're very globalist.

Brock: Real quick to Celeste. Now, Celeste, for those who don't know, you are a high-ranking officer in FEMA. That means you worked for the federal government. High level of clearance. There's so much you can tell us. And maybe you can't. You had shared things about why you left. Working, doing what you were doing, and you shared about what they were going to do to the Christians. Would you please share a little bit about some of those lines and how what you knew about their agenda of way before this COVID-19 got surprisingly released into the government? I mean to the world. Please share.

Celeste: Right. So right after 911, there was this big wave of patriotism. And what many people don't realize is that by the next day, there were huge programs out there. One is a volunteer program to federalize every single man, woman and child in America, turn them into slaves, basically a slave labor force. And basically.

Celeste: So, I was at task to do a particular job, and I could not do it spiritually, morally or ethically. I tried to say no, that was not an option. They were not taking no for an answer. And so basically, I left the agencies because it was that they knew what time was coming, which is what we're seeing now, that if you did not believe in the ideology of the state and that the state was God, that you would be incarcerated for a brief time. This is different than during the Holocaust. It would only be like a holding facility if you were re-educationable. If you had a particular task that you might be able to perform, you might be reeducated and reskilled. I guess what they call it now and reintegrated back into society. But for everybody else, you would be killed. And they thought it was rather funny. They were belly laughing about it. And it was at that point that I left the agencies. I went to my inner circle, said, "am I perceiving this right?" And they said, "you don't have any options. You need to leave." And so that's what I did. I did leave. And I would like to speak to the question about the forcing of the vaccination. Yes, I think it's very important I get this question an awful lot in our community. Like so each Christian, you listeners out there have need to do your due diligence. The Lord expects you to be understood, understand what's going on in the signs of the time. Remember how he scolded the Sadducees and the Pharisees, that they didn't understand the signs of the time? **And so, you need to know that we are in the end days, we are in the tribulation period.** And you are facing this vax, this abominable vaccination, **which I believe is the mark of the beast, because they are saying you will not be able to buy and sell, you will not be able**

to integrate into society unless you take this. So that is Revelation 13. So as a Christian, **what you need to do is not only think in your head and rebuke it, but you also need to verbally say, I stand against this. I cannot do this.** This is contrary to my religious belief. I am not compromising. And whatever consequence that you may get, if you're thrown in prison, if you're killed for it, and then it you stretch out your neck and you say, Jesus, like they did in the in the old like in the book of Esther, when she went before the king, you know, she was pleading for the Jewish people. She stretched out her neck and the guy could have just chopped off her head because she went before the king unannounced. **So, we have to stretch out our neck. And if we perish, we perish.** *We were born for such a time as this, we hold in our faith.* **But the Lord, if you could take a stand against this and you don't take a stand against it because you're a coward, God is not going to honor that.** Praise God. That's right. But let's say that you are forced like, you know, they knock you unconscious and they put it in you. The fallback that we have, and scripture tells us this promise is that we are a new creation in him. So, he is faithful to us. So, if we are forced, you know, if it's out of our control completely, we, you know, we're unconscious, whatever he's he will recreate us whatever damage and havoc he has the power he has the power of all creation. He comes in our mother's wombs. He is going to recreate us and nullify any of the effects. But if we are just sitting there, you know, mousey and saying, Oh, you know, I don't want to like, I don't want to do it, you know, if we're mousey about our faith, he's not going to have our backsides.

Celeste: We have to be bold in our faith. And he knows God is. We know that this is the mark when it says, you know, you can't buy or sell without it. It's mandatory. It's got all these abominations in it. You can't get much. The beast system's been launched. The Antichrist is about ready to be revealed. I mean, it can't get any clearer now. I do have questions about what about my infant children or what about a mentally ill person or, God forbid, somebody with, like, Alzheimer's. And they are given this. The Lord desires that all people be saved. And if you are not capable, if you do not have the cognition to make a conscious choice for Jesus Christ and draw that line in the sand and rebuke this mark, then he's not going to hold you accountable. Like he would not hold a newborn because they're not of age. Now, maybe you get over 13, you get of age to make decisions. You know, we all as parents and grandparents, we need. It's incumbent upon us to teach our children and grandchildren that we need to oppose this and that we also need to teach them, you know, that they need to accept Jesus as their perfect, their savior, so that they can go to heaven and be with us if, God forbid, something happens. And the same with like a mentally ill person, you know, there's mildly mentally ill people. And then there's people that are severely and like my moms in the last stage of Alzheimer's, she's got a strong body. She's strong as an ox, but she doesn't have a mind. And the Lord's not going to hold her responsible if they shoot her with this vaccine. Unfortunately, my mom has not made the choice for Jesus Christ. But I believe even unto your last breath, even as your spirit is going out to its permanent habitation, he gives you one last choice.

Celeste: I mean, that's just my personal belief because it says that he desires that all be saved. So that's kind of my take and that's what I've been sharing with people. But you really have to study what this vaccination is all about. **You have to openly rebuke it verbally.** You have to take stand against it with everything that you have because you know. It says, I mean, there's only two things that basically say you're going to be cut off and one is the mark, and the other is blaspheming the Holy Spirit.

Brock: Right. If we don't mind going back to Jeff, you know, I've watched a lot of Jeff's videos. And Jeff, would you mind telling everybody what God told you about the vaccine? Because it is the same as what Celeste is saying. You said that God told you not to do it. What else did God tell you about the vaccine, Jeff?

Jeff: Well, **the Lord told me not to even get tested for it for COVID 19**.

Celeste: Trump, the plan is, to test three million people every week in America alone. **This testing puts you in the Beast system database and they evaluate for Pre-crime/post-crime.**

- Post Crime - If you've ever like got a speeding ticket or a parking ticket that you didn't pay, child support, that type of thing.
- Pre-crime - like what is your spiritual condition? And they know and it's in the beast system thing.

Celeste: And three million people a week are going to be tested and that means you're constantly going to be tested as you go out in public. It's going to be like once a month you have to go get your coronavirus test. Well, I'm refusing it because I am a child of the living God. **And I don't want it. I refuse to be a part of the Beast system**. As a matter of fact, I just surrendered my cell phone, my Costco card, and my Amazon Prime account. This in this last week because I found out that they put the update on my phone. They automatically put contact tracing and in the fine print it says, oh, it's this contact tracing is considered essential information. If you ever touch your phone, it sends that straight to public health, straight to the system, everything that you do, all your contacts, everything. And that went with the Costco card and the Prime Amazon Prime two.

Laura:. People are already waking up, become aware of everything that's happening. And even the conspiracies that were conspiracies are not conspiracies anymore. People want to know. We want to know what to do next. What do we do as Christians, as the Bride coming to Christ? What do we do as the church?

Pamela: People need to make sure they're rock solid with their faith in Jesus because you're going to be led by the Holy Spirit every single day to know what to do. Literally those that are led by the Holy Spirit, they are the sons and daughters of God. That's how I live every single day, knowing that our we're living in God. Tell me what to do, tell me what to do. And He does.

Pamela: But let me say this. There are practical things. If you do not have long term healthy food supplies, you better go out and get them all to get good because **planned famine is coming.** It's a communist tactic. They've always used it to weaken a nation they're targeting to **make people comply or you don't get the food comply or die.** Practical things. People do get their food supplies now and forget what their FEMA says it's hoarding. The US military has hoarded up to ten years of emergency food supplies. Right now, the deep underground military bases knowing World War Three is coming and these things are coming. If they can do it, you sure can to.

Pamela: And you better feed your family, get your emergency vitamins, food, supplies, all your essential things. Because these will I know from years of research, talking with people, planners of the New World Order agenda, these things will be cut off and used to control people. **Hey, if you don't comply, take the mark.** If you don't do what you say, you don't get food, you don't get this, you don't get that. Get your food, supplies and all your practical things. Vitamins, get your survival emergency supplies together. Pray and ask God to lead you and stock up on them. Get your emergency bug out backpack if you can get out of the cities, get out. We've long been told the cities will be hit the worst and we're already seeing that now. As I was told, rioting and looting would break out and they would be deliberately triggering it to create maximum chaos. **And out of the chaos and the ashes of it bring forth a new world order.** So, you need to have food supplies, emergency supplies.

Jana: Okay. Well, you know, seek the Lord specifically for your family in the closet. Go to closet, pray and seek the Lord what to do it for your own family. And He will answer. I did that and I got answered through a dream. And I'm not publicly saying it because it's for me, but basically it was a dream about to prepare physically as well. Not only spiritual is number one, of course, but we just, like Pamela said, we have to prepare physically and just like my family is doing now, begin to relocate from this state to a little better area where it would be safer and where we can grow our own food. So, yes, have a supply of food. And I want to give you a little more information on how to buy food. Most people just buy canned food, and they buy a lot of stuff that is good for two years, maybe, or maybe three years or four years, some canned foods. But there is such a thing as mylar bags and oxygen absorbers.

Jana: You think of this: rice, beans, pasta, any kind of grain, and the seeds and the spices you can replace all of that with oxygen absorber, seal with an iron, and it will be good up to 10 to 15 years. So, pasta is good for two years. You just prolong the life up to ten years.

Steve: You're saving, you save money rather than ordering everything through these long-life companies.

Jana: Now remember, remember that if we do garden and gardening is wonderful and we will do our own gardening as well. We already started, but that might be prohibited by law.

Pamela: That's right.

Jana: So, think of how to get vitamins and its maybe seeds sprouting when you sprout seeds at home. It has sprouts and those sprouts are full of minerals and vitamins that you can consume for health.

Steve: There's one other thing to think about as well, and that is from the intelligence sources that I have. You need to prepare as if you're living in the 1700s so we're not going to have electricity or any of these things.

Pamela: That's right.

Steve: ... even widespread. That's not just for the Christians that's going be, they're doing that to cripple everybody and to break ...

Pamela: EMPs.

Steve: Exactly. And there is a thing called EMP Shield. I believe it does work. It will keep your car alive, but the thing is you're not going to have gas. That's not going to really matter. So, my thought ... It would be a good idea to have it in case, you don't want to get stranded. I know people specifically that have contracts with FEMA. They've been preparing them for over a decade now to haul the cars off the highways. But I would look at least solar panels, portable solar panels and some kind of EMP protection for those types of devices.

Steve: There are three different devices. I don't know what they are. I just know that that's the case. So, if you want to have some sort of electricity, you need to have somewhere to do that. **Forget the idea of a generator because the generator is not going to be any good if you've got to put gas in it unless you've got 1000 gallons of gas.**

Steve: Also, tools. I'm big into all the old manual style tools, including drills, not electric. Cordless would be okay if you have the solar panels but think about primitive type of tools.

Jana: Manual coffee grinder. You know, manual coffee.

Brock: You need coffee at the end of the world, right?

Pamela: Of course! And chocolate ♡

MY THOUGHTS:

Wow! This was our top-rated video! This is all a few months of when this broke up. May 2020. Each one of these speakers gave you valuable information that you need to know Bride!

PANEL DISCUSSION AT NOAHIDE LAW CONFERENCE W/DR. JUNE & BROCK KNIGHT, LYNN TAYLOR AND STEVEN BEN-NUN ON AUGUST 2021

Speaker #1 – Brock Knight

Speaker #2 - Dr. June Knight

Speaker #3 - Steven Ben-Nun

Speaker #4 - Lynne Taylor

Speaker1: Hello, everybody. I hope you're having a good night. This is the Noahide week.

Speaker2: I mean, this is the fruit of Jana's hard work and her efforts to bring it to the forefront about the Noahide Laws. And now it's here. I mean, it's like literally coming to pass. And we're just honored that we get to be a part of Jana's very hard work. And so, let's just all give Jana a big hand right now. **Thank you, Miss Jana!**

Speaker3: And of course, you know, the presidents have been signing annually the commitment on the birthday of Menachem Schneerson. They call him The Rebbe. It's not, they don't call him a Rabbi, but a Rebbe. **Rebbe has more of an elevated place of a rabbi.** And of course, they believe that Schneerson was also a messiah figure. And every year, in honor of his birthday, the presidents all the way going back, ahh, I don't remember for sure, but it was Reagan or Carter that it goes back to, but they would sign off on basically for the Noahide

Laws, but they would do it under during his birthday to honor him. He was still alive at the time when they started this. And, of course, though, Jana began to really in her research through different books and stuff and a lot of these books being written by Jewish authors and stuff, she began to realize the dangers that these Noahide Laws would create for Christians. And then she really began to dig deeper and deeper and deeper. And there were others that had brought this up before, but no one ever brought it out the way she did and really brought it up. I even remember Nehemia Gordon back maybe a few years before that, he was on with, I forget that guy's name. I know him actually personally, but it's just kind of slips my mind who he was, who he is. But Nehemia was on his program and the, the guy that was that was hosting him, he was a little skeptical, like it wasn't that big of a deal. But Nehemia said, No. It is a big deal. This is Noahide Laws. This is written by Rambam. You know, Rambam is a, I think an 11th century sage that or Jewish sage, the way we should say that during the time of Rashi Rambam as well and he had written in the Talmud he was part of his writings are in what we call the Midrash, and he writes about the law of the kings. And this is where the seven Noahide Laws appear at. But even in there in the writings there, the sub-laws that are added in there. And this, although they may look like the Ten Commandments, even though there only seven, it's the fact that the sub-laws, when it talks about the idolatry, of course, that's the goes against Christians. That's the one where Christians could easily be beheaded. And when Jana saw this and then saw how this would affect believers, she couldn't rest day or night.

And she did the research deeper and deeper, uncovering all the different rabbis' that were involved in this. Even with Dr. June Knight, you know, the contributions that she began to uncover as well, seeing what was going on with the president and the people that he was aligning himself with. So, I was really amazed because even our channel, because of the Noahide Laws on Israeli News Live on YouTube, our channel, even we had kind of stagnated and it luckily it was at a time when the COVID thing was starting off too when it really began to snowball effect. And so, when they started not using so much of their moderators to keep us suppressed in our and our subscribers, we just exploded and new subscribers. And literally, I guess we grew like 60,000 people or 70,000 people in a six-month period all because of the information she was trying to get to the Christian people that this is a major danger. And of course, at this time, **Trump's already president and she's seeing that Trump is going right along with the game plan of forcing the Noahide Laws upon the people.**

Speaker1: Well, with that being said, let's introduce Ms. Lynne Taylor here. Ms. Lynne, you are a homeschool, mother I would imagine, mother,

Speaker1: …Your children, and you began to look into the education. Can you give everyone here a little history of how that curtailed into you, and you read about the Noahide Laws and then speaking up about it?

Speaker4: Okay. All right. Well, thank you very much. Okay. So, yes, as a homeschool mom, I found out that globalism was sneaking into the homeschool community and I wanted to find out more because, you know, after all, being in a leadership position, I knew I needed to protect not only my family, but those who were in my circle of influence. So, I got to look in at how corrupt the government had become at overreaching into education. So, **I already knew that Jimmy Carter had signed the US Department of Education into being in 1979.** Now I'll come back to that, okay. I'll circle back to that. But in the meantime, I'm going down this trail of finding out, no, our government has been doing all kinds of things in education that they have no constitutional right to, no moral right to, and it's using we the people's taxpayer money to pull it all off. So, the stretch to globalism was not that hard to find. And it wasn't until this summer that one of the people who has been so great at sharing information with me said, "Hey, did you see this particular article out of Christian News that shows that the Chicago Public Schools are teaching nothing but Noahide Laws in their curriculum?" And I said no. And so, he knew how much of a research person I am. And so that's when I started looking at it. And then it was okay, **we've tied Noahide to not only to the Lubavitch movement, but we've tied it to the Vatican, which is part of the Catholic Church, which aligns with the United Nations.** I've been able to find out how the United Nations lock, stock and barrel agreed to carry the Noahide Laws. And here's where we're circling back to President Carter, because it was President Carter in 1978 who made that first proclamation.

And it was, of course, to celebrate what a supposed great leader, Rabbi Schneerson was and how our country needed to use education to make careers for jobs and use education to not only pump up the basic human right of being educated, but to use morals and ethics that were tied to the Noahide system, which are not laws. They are man-made, Talmud based principles that our nation has taken in. And here's where it gets even more interesting. All right. So, he does this in 1978, a year later.

Speaker1: Did you learn this in 1978?

Speaker4: No, no, no, no.

Speaker1: Yeah. Tell us the history. I was like, wow, you're okay. So, you just learned this this summer.

Speaker4: This is how, it was amazing how it all unfolded. **So, he does this in '78. A year later creates the Department of Education with the Noahide system already embedded into everything about education**. And it has been endorsed by every president from Carter up all the way to Trump.

Speaker2: Yes. That's right.

Speaker4: And what was really shocking to me was somebody pointed out, well, hey, in 1983, President Reagan made it the year of the Bible, but he, too, signed the proclamation. And what the proclamation is, is not so much celebrating this twisted individual as is saying, oh, this is education day and we're going to give education back to the world. Well, if you look at what is in this, **it's saying that these were these laws have been around since the dawn of civilization**. No, they haven't. They couldn't be because they were not from God. They are not in God's word. And this is why we've seen education use so much as a change agent, not only for how we think, but how we feel, how we worship, how we believe, where we go, what we do. This is meant to permeate every aspect of our lives, and they knew the global powers that be, knew education was the way to do it.

Speaker1: And you were homeschooling. So homeschooling parents are still affected by this?

Speaker4:   Absolutely. Yes. This is this is what the sustainable development goals from the United Nations, because they marry right into them. These are one of the ways that the Noahide is carried out. For example, no poverty. Well, in real time, that means you're under a nanny state which we're seeing unfold before our eyes. End hunger. **Well, in real time, you're replacing God made food with machine-based food.**

Speaker1: Hold on. Hang onto that. We don't want to give away all the goodies away yet.

Speaker4: All right. We can circle back.

Speaker1: Okay. All right. That's, that's, that's some good stuff. Hang on to that, because we're going to get on that because what I want to do, I want to get how Mom found into it. Then I want to have everybody define this. We're going to start from a foundation and have everybody to give more of a definition and catch people up with a foundation. And then we're going to kind of layer upon layer. And before anything, I do want to give a disclaimer. Listen very closely, everybody. Okay? First of all, we love God, and we love people. That means we love the Jewish people.

Speaker2: Yes.

Speaker1: We're not anti-Semitic at all. But listen, that depends on which government is defining it there, because we do preach the gospel.

Speaker2: That is true.

Speaker1: And we believe that Jews need to accept Jesus and that they become a new man, one man in Christ, the new man and circumcision availeth nothing. It's a new creature. It's a new man. Okay? And we lovingly speak that truth. Okay? So, what we're going to be doing is only talk about what is a movement out there. And it has been going on for a very long time.

And we're exposing, the people we're exposing just happened to have been Jewish. Okay? And thing and other people as well. But we're going to let you know we're going to be we have a disclaimer that we'll put out there officially. I just want to let you know that we are not out here trying to attack Jews. We're not. But we are going to expose something that affects all Gentiles, which is everyone that's not a Jew and it affects everybody in this world. So, you got to pay close attention now. So, Mom, Dr. June you are up at the White House, White House correspondent and I remember you sharing this that you all of a sudden just came smack face right in this Noahide Law just by happenstance. You just boom. It hits you. Can you share how you got in and how you discovered this?

Speaker2: Well, it goes back to when I traveled the country in the MAGA Revival tour in 2017. I went across the country pro-Trump, interviewing everybody. How do you feel about us having this Christian president? I traveled 36 states, 18,000 miles believing in this man. I mean, it wasn't for him. It was in obedience to God. But the point was, is I went across this country just so excited of, you know, this turnaround of our country and the patriotism that was back, you know, the love of country that we all have. And as I was out there, after about two or three months, I began to see something's not right. **You know, something in the underbelly, the undercurrent of the country is sick. The church is sick**. And so, after I finished the six-month tour, I got on my knees, I got in the prayer closet, and I was like, God, something is wrong. I wanted to quit ministry, actually, because I was trying to do unity so much and I was like, I don't want unity with that. So, I was very, very devastated. And I began to research, okay? See, this is a lot of people's problem. They don't research. I began to research. Okay. What is this that I'm seeing? **Because something has infiltrated the Bride. Something has caused her to be tainted so much that she can't even see it.** They'll get up on the platform half naked. They'll get up there with no thought of leaving their wife or their secretary and just, you know, it's just they've been so tainted by the enemy and they're so blinded. So, I began researching. Then I started on these four books. Then God sent me to Washington to finish the story. When I got to Washington, D.C., I went in there pro-Trump. I mean, I even yelled at him the first time I met him. I yelled at him, and I was like, "President Trump, we love you!" And he stopped and he goes, "Well, thank you." You know, but I believed in him so much. I was so disappointed when I began to see his partnership with the enemy and how the evangelicals, because I was up there with all of them, with all this, you know, circle I was in and their partnership with perversion and their partnership with Idols. Okay. Then when I started seeing the President come forward with his agenda of the LGBT and his agenda of taking our guns and against the church called the Extremist The White Supremacists, the extremist. Then my eyes became, became open and people were telling me, you need to look up Steven and Jana Ben-Nun. They will teach you about the Noahide Laws. And that's how I found them. And I'm sitting up there in the White House researching these people because of the knowledge that they had about the Noahide Laws. And then it began to make sense. So, the last few months that I was there, I traveled to the UN with the President, and I was in the back of the UN after walking through that satanic building. I can't even tell you how, I don't even know what they do in that building, Steve. I'm telling you I don't even want to even think about it because the creeps are not even the word how you feel in that building. It is just like the Lucifer's castle, you know? And so, I'm in this building and I'm looking down at the very man that works in the UN every day, pushing the Noahide Laws, which is nothing but the global unity. And he's sitting down there in front, in front of the president with all the evangelicals. And I just wanted to throw up. I'm like, you've got to be kidding. And they do all of this in the name of international religious freedom. But what they don't tell everybody is that additional two words that does the church in. It's called "And Belief" and that "and belief" is the LGBT and all the other like the Noahide, all the other partnerships. And so, they're sitting down there with these people and I'm like, "What the world?" So, God pulled me out of Washington and then I began coming out and this year because he pulled me out right before Corona and then, now in 2020 is when God put me together with you. And then we're just like you, Steve. 2020 was the year that God catapulted us out there and we began telling people the sickness that we're seeing in this deal with the Noahide Laws. And now I'm just going to tell all of you, Bride, I've been following President Trump since this began with the coronavirus. And do you know this is where they're bringing in the Noahide Laws?

Speaker4: Uh huh.

Speaker2: **When they talk about natural law, and they talk about all the people coming together under this common unity and how all the moral decline of the country**. I mean, all you have to do is look at the conventions, the Republican convention and the Democratic Convention. They both spoke the same type of language of the changing of the foundations of our country, that we have went into such a moral decline, much less what has happened with the New Apostolic Reformation who is fighting for the foundations to be overturned and to come up into this new world and this utopia. So that's what brought me to this place.

Speaker1: My goodness. There's so much we can talk about. But let's just take everyone here on a quick synopsis of and I'll start on a little bit on this just for the sake of giving you guys a starting point because everyone knows here about the Bible, Old Testament, New Testament. You have the five books that Moses wrote, the Torah. Right?

Speaker2: Yes.

Speaker1: Right inside there you have the Ten Commandments. They come out of Egypt. They they're in the wilderness, Mount Sinai. We all know about the law that was given to Moses and like 613 commandments that go with it and everything like that and all the different things. And I could be saying some of those numbers are wrong, but basically you have the law given to Moses. But then there was this thing called the oral law, okay? Not the written law, the oral law, the Mishnah, right? And this is where we get oral tradition passed down. The Talmudic heritage or traditions of certain rabbis and whatnot. Now, Steve. With that being said, this oral law, so we're talking about the Noahide Laws, it's seven Commandments that basically are seven out of the ten that they are saying. They would tell you that these Seven Commandments came in the Book of Genesis before we were given the Mosaic laws before Abraham. So, Noah now in Genesis and Noah, he gave commandments to his sons. These are the Noahide Laws. And this is where they're saying that from the foundations of our world, from the very beginning, these commandments are stuff that even apply to Gentiles and everyone. But that's one thing they'll tell them as a good message because it makes sense to the normal person. Now, the other side is they're not telling them that **this is all nothing but rabbi traditional oral you know, the Talmud.** How they interpret scripture for many, many, many volumes back in Babylon is the first well written stuff. So would you like to give, with that being said, a definition and kind of define to us to no one's ever heard about Noahide Laws. What is the Noahide Laws?

Speaker3: Okay. Noahide Laws are, like you said, they do resemble that of some of the Ten Commandments like idolatry, you know. But things like don't eat the limb of a living animal, that's nowhere in the Ten Commandments.

Speaker 3: **So, but these come up in what we call Talmud, midrash, Mishnah, things like that.** There are different breakdowns of what we call the Talmud, which is, as you mentioned, this is what in Judaism they consider to be the oral law. You need to understand a little background on oral law, how that come to be, to really kind of grasp why the Jewish people believe this in the first place. There's a very obscure passage in the Old Testament, and I can I'll figure it out what it is a little bit and I'll share that passage with you. But the Jewish people use this particular passage to justify saying that God does not, He does not intervene on what's going here on the earth. He actually only he allows the rabbis to make those rules and laws, and which is not true. The passage that I'm speaking about, it doesn't even say that. But as a result, though, the Jewish people have believed this. And so therefore, they believe that the corrections and the add-ons and things like that to the Scripture is done by these rabbis' and that they have the authority to do so and that the Jewish people believe that. And I can't speak for all Jewish people because we have what we call Karaite Jews. And Karaite Jews literally believe in the Old Testament only. They do not believe in Talmudic law. They do not accept the mission of the Midrash or any of the other many different volumes of books that are written by rabbis. And so. So, you can't lump all Jews in the same category, but your orthodox believing Jews, and even in some other type of Jewish beliefs is that the oral law is handed down to the rabbis and they disseminate that to the rest of the public. The idea came up with Rambam is the one that actually put in what we call the law of Keynes in the Talmud. And this was about 1000 years ago that this was actually done. And he claimed and there is actually a book that was written by a man not too long ago. Rambam's idea was that when we when we read about the story, when God wanted to be the king over Israel, but Israel wanted a king anyway. They didn't want to go with God's plan of God sending a prophet to Israel. And at the time we had Samuel, the prophet on the scene. And so, when Samuel comes down and says, God wants to be your king, and but they said, we want a king like the rest of the nations to lead us into battle. But he said, you've upset God. So therefore, Rambam's idea was, okay. Samuel never wrote down what the law of the king was. And basically, it was supposed to be a law for Gentiles because they were going to have a king. And so therefore the Gentiles had their own laws. But the absurdity of this was he did write down what the law of the king was, because God actually tells Samuel, go back and tell them this is what's going to happen. Okay. I am your king. I am leading you. But if you want an earthly king, he's going to take your daughters for confectioneries, he is going to take your sons for foot soldiers. And then he lists the whole thing, has absolutely nothing to do with seven, as they call Noahide Laws. Now, of course, that was from the book of Samuel, but also when Rambam wrote this, he also takes it and claims that these laws too come from Noah. But when you go back and you read the story of Noah in Genesis, there are there are no seven laws that Noah speaks about. I mean, he does speak of a couple of different things. You know, you don't you know, you don't eat the blood of a living animal. You know, know this is where they get the kosher law. In other words, if you're going to eat the animal, you got to take all the blood out. You know, you're not to kill each other, you know. But Noah only mentions, I think, three different commandments, never seven. So, this is clearly something that was never needed. I mean, in fact, even a Gentile went by Ten Commandments, even though they may not be Jewish. We know this like in the case of when Abraham when Amalek wanted to take Abraham's wife and Abraham was afraid that the people would want his wife. So, he said, tell them that you're my sister. You know, why was he doing that? Because the law was and it was even amongst the Gentiles, he couldn't marry her because she had a husband. She and the husband were alive. But if the husband was dead, he knew he could be free to marry her. And this is why Abraham knew this. He knew that they'd believe that. So therefore, he said to her, you know, and this is conjecture, I guess I would have to say in that case there, but I think this is the reason why Abraham said tell him you're my sister because he didn't want to die. Because he knew if they found out his wife, they'd kill him so they could justify and say, well, her husband's dead. We'll marry like David did with Bathsheba, sends out Uriah to get killed. So that's kind of where that went to. And of course, they applied these laws to the Gentiles and not to Jews. Jews get the Ten Commandments and the 613, as they call them, Mitzvot or laws that are recorded in the Old Testament.

Speaker1: Ms. Lynne. Definition. How would you tell someone who's never heard of Noahide Laws, this is what the Noahide Laws are without telling them everything you know? How do you tell someone that asks you what are the Noahide Laws or Noahide movement?

Speaker4: Okay. I would basically say it is a movement that seeks to mock our Lord and Savior, to stress that there is no God or that there are many ways to God. Take your pick on which side you want to be on. I would also say that it is a movement that seeks to destroy Christianity. **It is a system that seeks to murder, to divide, to plunder, to control.** And its use in how it would impact education is that it's teaching that all these things are permissible. It's teaching that perversion is okay. It's teaching that manipulation of your attitudes; your values and your beliefs are okay. **Because as long as we can control what you think and how you learn, then we can have that global morality for the greater common good that is part of the United Nations message.**

Speaker1: All right, Mom. Same question to you. If someone asks you right now Noahide Laws. What in the world is the Noahide Laws? How would you answer?

Speaker2: Really, in a nutshell, **the Noahide Laws is the manmade solution to the problem because they do not want the church's solution. They don't want Christianity's solution to the problems of society.** So, they are inside of the UN which I told all of you is, is the body of the beast. **They want to give the body of the beast the solution to world unity.** That's why they have all these videos of world unity is through us we have the very basics of the laws that you need in order for us to be successful. And here's the thing. They tell everybody that we can all be in unity.

You know, if we just do away with everything past Noah's day, well, then you have to remember the scripture in the Bible that says in the **"As in the days of Noah"**.

Speaker1: Come on.

Speaker2: You know, you think of that as in the days of Noah, because they want to say you don't need Christianity because they're all supremacists. They think they're better than all the Jews because they're telling the Jews that they have to convert to Christianity, that they have to go to this new covenant over here in Christianity, and that our heaven is not good. So, they think they're suppressed. So, we're going to get rid of the New Testament and we're going to go all the way back to Noah. Which is why when you read these documents from the President and you understand, which is what I'm going to talk about today, the way that he's changing the educational system, using that to bring in the Noahide Laws. **So, basically the Noahide Laws in a nutshell, is where they are trying to give the moral answer to the problems that they don't want Christians to handle.**

Speaker1: All right. So, my turn. I'm going to use for the sake of giving everybody the last full picture here, I'm going to go to Google and give you guys what it is being said out there and then we'll summarize.

Speaker2: There you go. That's good.

Speaker1: Britannica. Okay? Noahide Laws. Judaism. Are also called Noachian Laws. That's a Jewish Talmudic designation for seven biblical laws given to Adam. And to Noah before the revelation to Moses on Mount Sinai. And consequently, because of that, it's binding on all mankind.

Speaker2: Wow.

Speaker3: Yeah.

Speaker1: So that's Britannica. Here's Wikipedia. In Judaism, the seven laws of Noah otherwise referred to as the Noahide Laws or the Noachian Laws are a set of imperatives which, according to the Talmud, were given by God as a binding set of universal moral laws for the sons of Noah. That is all of humanity. So, as you can see from the oral law, not the written law, the oral law, the rabbis' that wrote all of their interpretations of the written law basically turned into traditions, are in volumes of all kinds of books and however you want to say it scrolls called the Talmud or the Mishnah. Now these have what they call seven Noahide Laws that apply to not just the Jews, but really more towards Gentiles.

Speaker2: Yes.

Speaker1: These laws now are what we we're all right here saying what they are on a universal scale, on a mission to basically implement these laws to everyone in the world. Now, right now, currently, let's talk about, we'll talk about currently. Now, currently, we have the United Nations utilizing this. We have the Pope, we have Israel. They have now a Sanhedrin now, after thousands of years of not having it, we have the White House in the government. **All the countries in the world are implementing these Noahide Laws.** This is what we are going to share now, how this is affecting you. So now to go forward, we have education. We have the Israeli and the worldwide United Nations. We have the White House and president. And then maybe if I get a chance, I will share how it affects our church right now with the whole Jewish Roots and how we're being pulled in to believing this. And I've heard a lot, but I'm not going to get into it. Steve. Would you like to go in real right here and then let's, from that, from all the Talmudic things we've described now and the definitions, explain to us, the Rabbi Schneerson. Explain to us that he has done and his movement and how he is being honored and things like that. Then we'll flow into Lynne, because I know everyone here can go or might go to Mom.

Speaker2: No. You can take it.

Speaker1: All right. Please share with us on that, please.

Speaker3: Well, as far as Menachem Schneerson, you know, it really starts with him and the fact that he was revered to be the messiah. And but at the same time, one of the things that we've noticed about him is that it appears that he was more in line just from the things that he has said and **written of the Sabbatean Frankist doctrine, which is get things as evil as you possibly can to help usher in the coming of the messiah.** And I say that because, you know, like, for example, when he met with Netanyahu or Netanyahu met with him, Schneerson was asking him, what was he doing to help bring about the coming of the Messiah? And of course, Netanyahu says we're doing all that we can. He said, well, you're not doing enough. Do something more. He doesn't. He doesn't say specifically, you know, he's not encouraging him. But I mean, naturally, if you're Jewish and you hear something like this and we know the Sabbatean doctrine, which for those that don't understand the Frankist Sabbatean doctrine, this was the eviller you do, that that would create the scenario on the earth that would cause the messiah to come to fix the world and to set things in order. **Now, Christians should know that Jesus Christ was the Messiah, and he did come, and he did set the things in order.** But unfortunately, now that Christians are giving everything back to the Jews again, the beast is getting back his power. But in light of that, the Chabad community has built up a massive, one of the most politically minded organizations globally that affect every single government and entity in the world. I was part of Chabad. Now, keeping in mind that was not that I was Orthodox Jewish. It was because at that time still not having my eyes open to what Zionism was about, I happen to know a lot of Jewish people. I did business with a lot of Jewish people and then I got interested more into that side. So, I ended up getting involved there. So, I learned a lot of the inner workings of the things that went on. **The Schneerson, Rabbi Menachem Schneerson and I don't want to call him rabbi, but it's just for the sake of the title, we'd say, he was the man that spearheaded this massive globalist movement.** And just like the Vatican, the Vatican thinks centuries in advance on what they're going to do. So does the Jewish people as well. They think, you know, decades and decades in advance of the plans and the initiative and the global planning of what they're going to do to undermine this entire world. **And then if you begin to look, you'll see the tentacles of the Chabad movement is in every government that the Chief Rabbi of Russia is a Chabad. He's an American, actually, but he's Russia's chief rabbi.** And Putin is so sucked up with him. **You have Rabbi Cohen, I believe he's Chabad, who is the rabbi that Trump's very close to.** That's also…

Speaker2: That's the one I saw. That's right.

Speaker3: Exactly! **So, we have watched Schneerson pull together a global dominance.** And as you mention, the pope of Rome earlier, I believe that was Lynne that was talking about the Pope of Rome at the beginning of the broadcast, he literally, and I know this from people I know in the Pentagon that know specifically the details about this, he when he rejected the title of Vicar of Christ, which to me, no man is a replacement for Christ to begin with. But nonetheless, when he rejected that role and then I was told that the, this mantle thing that is heavily the most heavily guarded relic in the Catholic Church is that placard or whatever you want to call it that says that the pope of Rome is the Vicar of Christ, and this disappeared! It totally has disappeared, and nobody knows where it went. And of course, the Pope rejects that title. But as I was told from inside government officials, **the reason he did this was because he was submitting himself underneath Jewish authority that that the law was going to come through Israel, through Jerusalem, and that they had that he had to go underneath the rabbis' and he could no longer hold that title as a result, which we already know that he was heavily involved.** The, the Jewish community, the rabbis in Israel, he was already working with them when **Pope Francis before he was Pope, when he was yet a cardinal, he was sending archbishops to Israel to study underneath the Noahide.** I can't think of the name of the school, Jana would know, she's got a good memory on these things there. But there was just outside of Jerusalem, they were studying the Noahide Laws and how to take and become true Noahides. **And of course, the Pope of Rome has is clearly submitted underneath this rulership showing that the One World Government and the One World Religion is all going to be headed by Israel.**

Speaker1: All right. So, we're going to go to Lynn now. You had talked about this in our talk that we did, and we'll be uploading her teaching here, I think, tonight after this or in the morning.

Speaker4: Okay. All right. Well, let's see here. One of the things that I wanted to point out was, yes, **it was Carter who made the first proclamation to embed the Noahide Laws in education**. But it wasn't until Bush first who made it into a public law. And if you read the verbiage of that particular public law, you will see that education, one more time is taught as a basic human right, and that, of course, morals and ethics have to go in with this particular set of beliefs. Now, what I want to point out was the UN preaches education as a basic human right, and nowhere is it in our Constitution, our Declaration, our Bill of Rights. It's not even in the Bible that it is a basic human right. What was taught in the Bible was that parents were to teach and train up their children. That's in the Old Testament. The New Testament comes in Jesus was modeled as the ultimate teacher. He did not sit there and mandate how teaching should be. He did not do it under compulsory measures. He did not even say it was a basic human right. **So, this is a false teaching not only from Noahide but from the United Nations as well.** As far as the morals and the characters, again, go back to the Bible, that is the parents' responsibility. That is also part of the churches walking alongside the parents. But we're seeing that churches have sold out to this Noahide system as well. And when the United Nations married up with the Noahide union, it made it very apparent that the only way that a child could ever have true morals and true ethics are through the 17 Sustainable Development Goals. Now, very quickly, I want to share what that means in real time. I'm not going to tell you what the Sustainable Development Goals are, because anybody can go and find that out.

But in real time for poverty an anti-state control people in every possible way, including your education, your housing, your food and your medicine. We're seeing this play out under the Trump administration.

Speaker2: That's right. Amen

Speaker4: They tried in real time. For number two, we're replacing God made food with lab created. We're even having militant children come up and tell us, oh, you can't eat meat because meat is evil. Meat harms the planet. Meat is a bad climate change tool.

Speaker1: So meatless meat, right?

Speaker4: Absolutely. For your health care, which includes mental health, which goes back into education for social and emotional manipulation. It's not learning, it's manipulation. This is going to include mass overmedication. And where are we right now?

Speaker4: Where are we right now? Number four, supposed to be quality education for all. It should be quality indoctrination for all, barely academic based education, which is what it was supposed to be in the first place. Because if you look at the definition for education, it is a passing on of knowledge and skills. It is not workforce based, trained minions to a Noahide system that hearkens back to Karl Marx, who was also a Jew,

Speaker2: Wow.

Speaker4: ...that followed this movement and can be found in the Communist Manifesto, which...

Speaker2: Wow.

Speaker4: ...which we are living out in our nation right now.

Speaker1: Yup.

Speaker4: For gender, we're seeing a bully pulpit created and we're seeing how genders are being demonized. We're seeing how marriage is being put down. All right? Sustainable water in real time, your water will be totally controlled. If you control food and the water, you control people. Okay? **The Green Movement is also a bully pulpit, and it will rape the land, harm the environment more than what it's doing now and put people second to the earth. So, in other words, there'll be Earth worship, which we're seeing really pick up.**

Speaker2: Wow.

Speaker4: Jobs for all ties back into this indoctrination of our education because the government controls what you learn, where you work, how you live.

It kills the free market and manipulates a people and our economy. And what are we seeing now? All right. Resilient infrastructure, number 9. In real time, you kill the cash, which we are seeing happen.

Speaker2: Yes.

Speaker4: You align to the World Bank. You're digitally managed. Reducing Inequalities. This is another Sustainable Development Goal. In real time, you redistribute the wealth, and you create a caste system which this Noahide Law absolutely does. Sustainable Cities. In real time we force relocation to overcrowd, highly trackable cities. **So, in other words, if you live in the country, forget it, because that land will be taken over for things like the solar panels which harm the environment and the wind tunnels which kill the birds.** So, we're going to see a lot of things like that. All right. In real time for number 12, **you punish people via taxation, and you use social credit to track and reward or punish.**

Speaker4: Yes. And that's already in the works here in the United States under our current administration. It started, didn't start with the current administration. It's just coming to fruition. All right. Climate Change. All right. In real time, we're seeing a false narrative that drives legislations and laws like the United States-Canada-Mexico agreement that will set up Noahide like international councils over every aspect of our lives. Number 14, real time.

Speaker2: Preach it woman!

Speaker4: Real time realization of that one government control use of your food supply.

Speaker2: We're seeing that right now.

Speaker4: We're seeing that right now. All right. Number 15, Sustainable Land. In real time. **This means that private property ownership goes the way of the wind, and the government comes in and takes everything they possibly can.** Sixteen is supposed to be about peace and justice for all, which supposedly Noahide is all about. All right. **In real time, again, the social justice and the credit and mass chaos will ensue.** In number 17, the partnerships to make all this happen, you can trace to the Federal Reserve. You can trace to the Nature Conservatory. You can trace to our government. You can trace to United Nations, the church at large. You can trace it to every huge corporation out there who has a dog in this fight.

Speaker1: My Gosh. She's got a lot more where that came from. So, get ready.

Speaker2: Excellent teaching about that. That is so true.

Speaker1: We'll be putting a lot of that in. Now, Mom. Now, she brought up this, the United Nations.

Now, guys, we will in our talks, we are putting out every single thing the United Nations did. Basically, that was clearly stating they signed the declaration. They have signed things saying the Noahide Laws is basically, I'm not going to get into that yet. But from the White House, most people that are for Trump would never imagine that he would have anything sinister going on in the background because obviously he sacrificed his whole life to be our savior, to be our hero. Now, what would you say about what your experience is and what do you have here for us to share concerning this? Now, do you want me to share this really quick before I do that?

Speaker2: Go ahead.

Speaker1: I just want you guys to see something. I'm not going to share my screen here. I'm just going to read something for you. So, the founder and the Chairman of World Economic Forum, he has a…

Speaker2: Brain of the beast.

Speaker3: He has a big quote out there. Okay. And he's all about the Noahide Laws. He is an implementation master of this. Listen to this. He is right now they are marketing signs and everything and banners out there saying this, **"You'll own nothing, and you'll be happy about it." This is the New World Order. The great reset he's talking about. He is saying you'll own nothing like you will own nothing and you'll be happy about it!**

Speaker2: The reason is, is because everything is going to go over to stakeholders. I've been trying to teach you this, and I brought out last night that news broadcast we did last night was the best we've ever done. Y'all have got to see last night because we actually put the hammer on the nail when it comes to the agenda of the globe and what they're doing right now with the UN, with the president. I'm telling you, Bride, you've got to because we proved everything. We it was a three-hour broadcast, but we proved everything we said. And that is what they're doing is trying to make everything universalist is to everything is for the common good. Everything is shared. There is their doing away with capitalism.

Speaker4: Oh, yeah.

Speaker2: You know, they don't want anybody to be supreme anymore. Sharing the wealth. Sharing the wealth. What was you saying, Steve?

Speaker3: Except for those politicians at the top, they're going to stay supreme.

Speaker4: Yeah. And the corporations that got them there as well. But I just wanted to point out one thing to the to the listeners and to those who will watch this in the archives. This research is out there for anyone to access. You have to want to protect your family. **And if you're complacent, this will eat you alive.**

So, what we're what we're all bringing to the table is not stuff that is exclusive to us. This is out there…

Speaker2: Oh, yes.

Speaker4: For every American for every person who is listening outside of America who wants to know what's going on.

Speaker2: Okay. Going back to Brock's question, what you asked me.

Speaker1: I'm going to transition to you. I got to read this, and I'm done. I just got you to listen.

Speaker2: Go, Brock.

Speaker1: Listen. Welcome to 2030. This is World Economic Forum. Welcome to 2030. I own nothing. I have no privacy and life has never been better. These are the things they are literally marketing out there. No, I'm not kidding.

Speaker4: These are being taught to our children.

Speaker2: Yes.

Speaker1: This is the stuff you have out there now, Mom? Could that be happening in America? What do you got for us?

Speaker2: Well, the reason that they're saying that is because everything will be shared. And everybody will be transparent, and they won't nobody better than anybody else. So, everything will just be equal type of deal. But what I want you to know, Bride, about the Noahide Laws is what is happening in the White House. **There is a shifting in the foundations of our country that's taking place not only with the New Apostolic Reformation Church, which is partnered around the president. Okay. They are changing the foundation of the church. They want to flip the church over to this new order.** Okay. In the White House and in the government aspect of the United States, they are flipping everything under the order of the UN and one of the biggest clues of us going underneath the UN rule to me, I know Steve and Jana, I know ya'll said that on March the 13th, whenever all this started, that's when we lost America or whatever. **But in my interpretation is when he did the executive order on the UN Day.** And Bride, I just wanted to cry. In that order when I read, I read these things to you. When I read it to you, **he's basically saying we're putting the United States underneath the UN rule is the way I took it because he was talking about how very noble, they are and how their international law is so great and how we need every governor across this country to begin celebrating the UN, the United Nations.** And then with the way that he's doing our education and changing our foundational history to where he's changing the history books, Bride! I am looking right here a printed executive order by our president, and it's called **Establishing the President's Advisory 1776 Commission**.

And look right here, Steve. It says in Section One, The Purpose. **The American founding envisioned a political order in harmony with the design of the laws of nature and nature's god. And that right there tells you Noahide Laws**.

Speaker3: Yes.

Speaker2: When you understand. And then he says, saying the rights to life, liberty and the pursuit of happiness as embodied in and sanctioned by natural law. And see what gets you. Because I've got so many notes and I went through this whole thing, and I ripped it to shreds when we did that live.

Speaker4: Right.

Speaker2: You see, when I see this, it causes me to pause. It causes me to say, Oh, my gosh. I mean, he's literally taking Christianity right out right out the door, because he is saying in these documents that he wants everything to be equal and to quit saying that it's a Christian nation. And according to his paperwork, this will no longer be one people's nation. It's not going to be that way. It's going to be ecumenical. It's going to be everybody is going to have a shared vested interest and the fact that we're going global. And that we are now one big global community. But see, the thing is, is that since the New Apostolic Reformation has got all of the church snowed, now they can't see the forest for the trees.

Speaker4: Right.

Speaker3: That's right.

Speaker2: So, he can get up there and he can literally say, you know, stab you in the back 1000 times and they will not hear it. You know, it's like he he's completely changing the entire infrastructure, changing the entire nation. And he's free to do it because he has the church behind him. But who else do you know, Brock? That did the very same thing?

Speaker1: Hitler.

Speaker4: If I may just interject a couple of things to that that you were talking about, June. I did a show on that particular executive proclamation on the UN.

Speaker2: Because it was that offensive.

Speaker1: Yeah, it was that offensive.

Speaker2: To the Christians.

Speaker4: Right. Absolutely. And not only does it bring in the Noahide Laws, but let's remember, under the Constitution, a lot of these things that supposedly Trump is putting into action are not his jurisdiction. They have not been assigned to him. He was never supposed to create jobs, fix the economy. **He wasn't supposed to do all that. That is up to Congress. So, we're seeing we're seeing the president do something that no other president has done before and that is become an actual tyrant in front of us.**

Speaker2: Yes, that's absolutely true, because when I read you his executive orders. Bride, I'm like, What the world? He completely went by Congress. He, he completely, and the thing was for the LGBT. Steve, that H.R. 5 Bill, which was the worst bill for the LGBT against the church which came through House last year in May of 2019. Okay. Now, the president said back then, Well I don't want to approve it just because, you know, I don't really like the language. So, here's what he does, Bride. A year and six months later he turns around and does it his own self in an executive order and completely bypasses the House and the Senate…

Speaker4: Now what…

Speaker2: And changes the laws for the LGBT.

Speaker4: Now, what people need to understand is that if you look at the definition of what an executive order is, it is supposed to be an order that impacts only the executive branch of the government. It is never supposed to enact policy or create law or mandates, but mandates are not law.

Speaker2: And this is why we have checks and balances.

Speaker1: Right.

Speaker4: But this is why I'm saying we are seeing a tyrant come to rise right before us.

Speaker2: Now, Steve, can you explain to everybody how the Noahide Laws has so much to do with this change in the government that we see happening right now?

Speaker3: Well, here's what let me just say this, because you have to understand, Trump is only the puppet.

Speaker4: Right.

Speaker3: He's on strings. Every executive order he signs, they let him be the dirty guy to look like the tyrant. But in reality, he's really not that guy. It is, it is a masquerade behind there. And of course, it's that little country south of Lebanon that is pulling his strings to dictate these mandates that are going to go forth. And they are this too, you see with the election process, we see such a major conflict arising out of it. The left media, which also is controlled by that little country south of Lebanon, they are pumping up, getting the minority community so inflamed over Trump not conceding.

And believe me, I'm sure Trump would just like to go home, be done with all this, you know? They chose him maybe because of his narcissistic ways to play this part, I don't know. **But the thing is, he was chosen for this purpose, just like Obama was chosen…**

Speaker2: That's right. Amen. Yes.

Speaker3: …by Kissinger and groomed by Kissinger. **Literally, he was groomed by Kissinger to be the president of the United States.** The thing is, the, the entire agenda right now, in order to bring about all the things even like what Lynn was saying, that these changes that they're going to make, whether it be the sustainability, all these different laws that they're passing, they're gonna take your lands, things like that, they've got to collapse this nation to be able to do it. They've got to create a calamity here that is so massive.

Speaker2: Yeah.

Speaker3: I hate to say that. I mean, I don't want Biden to win either. I mean, let's just face it. It doesn't matter which one you get.

Speaker2: That's right. Amen.

Speaker3: You still have the evil. As my wife always says, people say, well, I'm going to vote for the lesser of two evils. She said, do you really think he's not this kind of evil? No. You know?

Speaker4: Thank you for clarifying that about you know, the tyrant and all that, Steve.

Speaker3: That's right.

Speaker1: He said to abhor, shun evil.

Speaker1: All right. I hope everybody understands so far pretty good a summary and foundation of what the Noahide Laws are and the threat they pose. Now, a lot of explanations will be broken down as we go throughout the week. Here's a question. My sister is a teacher's aide at an elementary school. She's with the kindergarten kid, but still sees what is going on in the school. What are some things that I can talk to her about as far as what to look for? They're probably not going to come right out and tell people, oh, by the way, we're going to start teaching the children about the Noahide Laws. Can you give some examples of the verbiage they may use? This way I can give her a heads up to keep her eyes and ears open to these things.

Speaker4: All right.

Speaker1: How about Lynn on that one? Education.

Speaker4: All right. Some of the things to look for as far as verbiage and signs. **Collectivism,** you know, how is your what does your family believe? Do they make you go to church?

Do you like going to church? What did you do if you didn't have to go to church? These are some of the questions that they start asking little people. They also ask, you know, hey, we're going to start talking about how we're all in this together. Well, yes, we've heard that through this kind of stuff.

Speaker2: Yes.

Speaker4: But they're starting to teach children younger and younger of this comprehensive sexuality stuff. So as young as kindergarten, you know, hey, here are your body parts. Now in kindergarten, you don't know really what your belly button is for, but you're supposed to be able to know what your, your God given genitals are for. No. Too much. Too soon.

Speaker2: Wow. That is sad.

Speaker4: You also need to start looking at what is being taught about creation. Is it that God is our Creator or that the Earth is somehow just all its own creation and that we, as good citizens need to adhere to climate change or take good care of the earth? Because again, this is starting out in not just kindergarten. This is going into daycare centers now.

Speaker2: What?

Speaker4: Uh huh.

Speaker1: And don't forget, Christian VBS.

Speaker4: Oh, yes, I have done some research and there is actually the church, on church schools. They love to bring in this kind of globalism that is tied to the Noahide Laws. We can find it in not only our Christian schools, our Catholic schools, you can also find it that there was a church in Virginia, I believe it was a few years ago, did a globalization VBS that was tied to all this kind of stuff.

Speaker2: Oh, no, thank you.

Speaker1: So, if you want to learn some more details on that, when we upload the training Ms. Taylor did today, when we upload that, you'll get more details on that. So, she goes into that.

Speaker1: Alright. Next question. Hi. My question is, how do I explain to my family about the Noahide Laws in a very simple way, so they get how important is it without freaking them out?

Speaker1: God bless you all. Now, we covered that earlier with Steve. You are sharing this more than all of us, I imagine…

Speaker2: How do you tell your family?

Speaker1: Simple.

Speaker4: But not freak them out?

Speaker2: Yeah.

Speaker1: Or is the strategy to freak them out, simply?

All laugh.

Speaker1: That was a good one.

Speaker3: Here, let's put it simple. You just kind of go like this, you know? Say, well, you see the conspiracy theories about all the guillotines that have been ordered and stuff like that?

Speaker2: Right.

Speaker3: Well, now, even the Canadian government it has been leaked out that, yes, they did order the yellow teams over in Canada as well. But I know for a fact as well that they were ordered in America and how they were ordered and how many blades were ordered. A million of blades were ordered of guillotines. And then you just simply say, Well by the way, it's kind of weird we get all these conspiracy theories out here about all these guillotines, and yeah, there might be some truth to it.

But isn't it kind of interesting that this Noahide Law, the sub law decapitates that Christian if you believe that Jesus is the son of God or however you want to believe? Okay. No, no, There's no easy way to say it, I guess.

Laughter.

Speaker3: But it's simple. But really and truly, sometimes you need to be shocked a little bit. And, you know, I think, though, in all sincerity, what people need to do when they're trying to explain this to their family members is that I would first show them how that this looks so innocent. And the Noahide Laws do look innocent. They appear on the surface...

Speaker1: Oh yeah.

Speaker3: that just like the Ten Commandments. Yeah. Nobody. I mean, idolatry is against the Ten Commandments. See, but the thing that you need to see, though, is that I want you to take and then show them what the interpretation is and who has the power of interpretation. And then if you can show them that, which, of course, it is the Orthodox community, and then you could build upon that and show them how that you have Evangelical Messianic teachers trying to put you underneath these rabbis in Israel as Christians that the law is supposed to come out of Jerusalem, which it did. Jesus Christ was that law.

He was that new covenant that Moses spoke about. But you have to show them how that there is a movement to place all Christians underneath the Talmudic rabbis' which Jesus says if they don't believe him, we know already know what he says about that but. And then once they can see that, then they can begin to realize there's something is up because in their sub laws of the Noahide Laws, they're going to behead you because of your faith in Jesus Christ. And then you can try to get them to understand that there is an agenda, and everything politically is beginning, and everything globally is beginning to line up with that agenda. No matter how they dress it up. Yeah. There is a natural law. A natural law that God set in order. But they stole that terminology and applied it to this to make it more palatable...

Speaker2: Right.

Speaker3: ...for the Christian community to accept.

Speaker1: Steve, where can you or someone that's listening research the sub laws so anyone who researches goes to noahide.org or noahide.com?

Speaker2: Oh, Noahide.org.

Speaker1: So Noahide.org. You can go on there right now and read it and says wow, this is wonderful. It makes sense. That's definitely Noah. That sounds like Christian.

You know, naive people will read that. How do you go and find sub laws?

Speaker3: You can actually, and I'll see if I can't get a link that we can include for the listeners and everything. But you have to understand the Jewish people they're not afraid to tell you what they are.

Speaker1: Hiding in plain sight all the time.

Speaker3: This would be a good avenue as well because when Jana speaks about things, she sources every single thing that there is and so there are Noahide.org. like you said, their website, their no idolatry, for example, and then they give some of the sub laws against entertaining the thought of there exist a deity except Hashem negative that is considered a negative mitzvah against making any graven image against having anyone else make one for us. And by the way, they are in the Talmud when you and you can't. But it's not going to work if you have the Encino Talmud is what I have. And this gives you all the breakdowns of those sub laws. But even since then, even since this has been written then, more rabbis continually add on even more sub laws. So, it really takes a lot of work. No, that didn't have they didn't have the sub laws there. And if you go to Moshe Weiner, who has in his book called *The Divine Code*, that book there will have all the sub laws in it. And he's a Jewish man that wrote the book.

Speaker3: *The Divine Code*. And it is a very thick book, but it is unbelievable amount of information. You see, the Jewish people used to hide these things from the public. These were very secretive things. You know? I mean, I can remember sitting with other very elite type of Jewish people's, doctors, lawyers, things like that that I knew personally, and they would always joke about Gentiles becoming slaves and stuff. And I really never took it seriously. I always thought, Okay, yeah right. You know always talking, We're going to enslave Christians one day. But it wasn't a joke for them. They were very serious about it.

Speaker1: All right.

Speaker3: But keep in mind that not all Jewish people are this way. And this is really I always like to say that because unfortunately, a lot of a lot of the people that expose the things that are really happening inside these circles are Jewish people that care about humanity. And even though they may not believe Christianity, they still care about Christians and what's going to happen. And they have come out and they try to expose these things. And so, we got always remember that. And then of course, you got secular Jews that don't care about it either. You know, they just want people to be able to live in peace together. Ahh, but unfortunately, there is a side that is bent on a much more sinister plan.

Speaker2: Yeah.

Speaker1: Do you think those presidents that signed these things in the law or have made an Education Day and know all the different proclamations, do you think they knew how sinister it was?

Speaker2: That's a good question.

Speaker3: You know, in some cases, I would probably have to say no. But then there's another side of me, though. You have to keep in mind. **You don't become president unless your part of some family, some there's a connection for every person that becomes president.** Probably one of the very few that was really not connected. But and I know this story for a fact was Ronald Reagan. **Ronald Reagan got in through popularity, but once the elites saw that there was a good chance, he would be president, this is when they demanded that he have Bush Senior to be his vice president because they needed to be able to control him.** And I know that Reagan was always interested in a lot of things like Area 51, things like that alien agenda. But they would never allow him to know anything whatsoever about this information. They said he did not have the security clearance that would give him authorization to be a part of any of that. That lets you know just that they're still controlled. And **that's why even with Trump sometimes, you know, there's a reason why he was chosen.** I don't really know the answer to for his reasons by that. **But still, he's the puppet on the strings.**

Speaker1: All right.

Speaker4: So, can I, can I add to the question about the presidents? All right. We know that Carter put into action the US Department of Education that was based on the Noahide. We also know that right after that Reagan came in. He could have disbanded the Department of Education and didn't for whatever reasons.

Speaker3: He would have been killed.

Speaker4: George W Bush…

Speaker1: He would have been killed.

Speaker4: He would have… Okay. We have George W Bush who made the New World Order declaration. You have Clinton who came up with the *Goals 2000* which took the caste system and put it into education through workforce training. We have Bush the 2nd *No Child Left Behind*, which really made education even worse. Then we had Obama, who signed Every *Student Succeeds Act* as well as the *STEM Act*, which supposedly was supposed to give control back to the States. But no, in fact, it increased the federal footprint in education, and we have seen the president continue every bit of this.

Speaker4: So that would be why I would say yes and no to these presidents.

Speaker1: Yeah, there's one way or the other to get a president to do something, huh? They do it willfully, knowingly.

Speaker3: You gotta keep in mind, too, when we talk about the presidents did this, they did that, they did this, they did that. They don't actually do any of it. This is not their own ideas. This is the ideas that are given to them. That's why they have so many advisors and stuff. It's the people that are in the background. And I know that we have **what we call level four, which really is there's different families at different levels and there's different families that people don't even know Rothschilds, Rockefellers, people like that. They're level four, level five.** But then you go higher ups and stuff, and these things are disseminated down. And that's why I know these presidents, other than you might have a president that is a brilliant individual that probably is smarter. Now, I do know Bush Senior. He was one of those. He was unlike other presidents. You know, Jimmy Carter, the peanut picker out there, you know, a little different with him. But when it comes to Bush senior, he is very very much involved knowing what's going on in the background and stuff. And that's why he was placed where he was placed and why he became president later. **He would probably be one that I would say knew what was going on.**

Speaker4: Okay. So, during each of these presidents' administrations. Then we'll put it that way.

Speaker3: Yes.

Speaker1: All right. So, this is a twofold question. Are the Noahide Laws in place now and when could or do you think, I guess, prophecy or whatever could the Noahide Laws go into full effect?

Speaker2: The timeline. Yes.

Speaker3: Well, I personally think that the full effect is **when they are able to collapse everything and then they bring out their new world order agenda. That will be the dawning of their new age.** And of course, it will, because you have to understand, Israel has to have their messiah figure, they have to have their messiah on the scene, and of course, **there has to be a major attack against the Christian people.** There's going to be a, you know because in Judaism, I shouldn't say it that way. **In some of these elite circles, they believe that that Ishmael has got to kill off Esau, but that's the Muslims against the Christians. And then the Messiah can come.** And to usher in this peace, this millennial reign. And they also believe that the Mahdi will begin to work with the Messiah to help usher this in. But already know they got both guys are in the waiting. I mean, these are things that, you know, from the circles that you that, you know, these people in, they can tell you about what's going on. So, they're ready for this to happen, but they're waiting for the calamity in order to bring it about. **So, yes, that's when you know the Noahide Laws will be in full force.**

Speaker3: All right, here's another are some other questions. So. All right. The Sanhedrin. Now, one thing we haven't brought up yet in this is that in the Noahide Law, they teach the last one or sometimes not the last, but the justice. Okay? So, they have these world courts, and they say that there needs to be a Sanhedrin in place. Now we know that in the Temple Mount a Sanhedrin meets now. So, can you explain the tie of Sanhedrin with this justice, which would be how our heads get cut off and things like that? Secondly, how would that Sanhedrin tie in with the International Courts that the UN has? Would they be the ones behind the scenes pulling all the strings, and that rhymes. Did you hear that? About the flow of that?

Speaker3: There is maybe differing opinions on how this would actually work out. I know there are some that believe that the Sanhedrin will actually replace the United Nations. I can see where that could possibly actually happen, especially once we have a New World Order. **But then I also can see to a possibility that the United Nations will end up working hand in hand where the Sanhedrin would take the lead role and it would be delegated down to the United Nations.** Because you have to understand the 21st degree Mason is considered to be the executioner of the Noahide Laws. The 21st degree Mason is called a Noachide spelled with a c h i d e which is another way that that it is spelled in Israeli circles. But and of course, their garb is a full executioner with a black hood, with a sword, etc. Ah, so, maybe they work under that mandate of the UN if the UN still stays intact and somehow or another.

MY THOUGHTS:

Bride, there is so much more interviews I have to share but I will stop here. This information in this book provides you with great information for you to make wise decisions and to inform your family and friends. Thank you to all the people we presented on here:

Steve & Jana Ben-Nun

Lynn Taylor

Pamela Schuffert

Celeste Solum

Jeff Byerly

Disclaimer: Just because I interviewed these people years ago does not mean I endorse their current beliefs or any beliefs. This insertion in this book is because they are experts in their fields at that time and I wanted you to know about the Noahide Laws and the evil one world order agenda. I do agree with almost all of their assessments though. Trust in the Holy Spirit to lead you into all the truth.

God bless you, Bride!

3

PRAYER

Dear Jesus,

Please examine my heart and let me know if I have participated in anything that hurts your heart. Please forgive me and I renounce any allegiance I have made with the devil. I renounce the Hebrew Roots movement and I embrace your faith, love, joy and peace. I want you to fill me with the Holy Ghost and power. I want a life of faith and joy. Deliver me of all unrighteousness and heal me, Lord.

I forgive all my sisters and brothers in Christ who have abandoned the faith. I release them to you Lord. Please show them the way. Help me to be a light unto my brothers and sisters in this dark hour.

Lord use me for your glory in this last hour and please help me to endure until the end. I cannot do it without you. I am utterly dependent upon you. I surrender all and the will of the Lord be done in my life. I give you all of me. I want to honor you with my life and the rest of my destiny here on Earth. Use me for your glory. In Jesus name. Amen.

This is the agenda in a nutshell.

ABOUT THE AUTHOR

We Are the Bride Ministries Founder

Dr. June Dawn Knight is a White House Correspondent, pastor, author, media specialist, mother and grandmother. Her heart is to serve her community. She has been in public service for the last 25 years. She spearheaded four organizations. The Middle Tennessee Jr. League Cheerleader's Association in which she unified four different counties and ten cities for cheerleading. MTJLCA still exists today. She also served as the president of the Steelworker's Union for the CMCSS Bus Drivers in 2004/2005. Then, she went to World Harvest Bible College in Columbus, Ohio. Following Bible College, she attended APSU from 2008 – 2012. During her time at APSU, she spearheaded three organizations on campus. Dr. June Dawn served student life and served on the Provost Committee for the students.

Dr. June Dawn graduated APSU in December 2012 with her master's Degree in Corporate Communication. She studied in London during Grad School under the top three global Public Relations/Advertising Firms in the world. During this time under the instruction of the University of Kentucky, she made a 100 in the class. She graduated with a 3.74 GPA. Dr. June Dawn had dreams of traveling the world for a major corporation, however, after graduation, God stopped her plans and called her back to the ministry.

Through the years Dr. June, as she is fondly referred to, has spearheaded multiple organizations that bring people together and give them a platform; many of which continue to function today. Additionally, Dr. June has served in multiple ministries all over the world working alongside visionaries to assist them in clearly defining, articulating and supporting implemental strategies that reflect and maximize the effectiveness of their Godly calling.

Currently as the CEO and president of WATB ministries, she has an astute ability to see through the deception that is unfolding in the world, along with an approach of reporting truth unlike any of our time. Her knowledge, experience and wit combined provide material that is godly, informative and life-changing for so many across the globe.

From London to the White House, Dr. June has been on an extraordinary journey to discover the heart of the spiritual condition of the country. The Lord intertwined her within ministries all over to give her a birds-eye view of ministry in today's culture. As the Lord sent her to the White House, remains a representative of the true church on a global level. She has the global picture of the church's situation and condition with the Lord.

Through the years of suffering, traveling and serving, Dr. June represented the Bride of Christ at the White House with truth and grace. The assignment there only lasted a year (the last year of America 2018-2019). Following this assignment, the Lord brought her back to Tennessee where she is now with her family.

Now she writes books about what she has learned in order to

help the Bride.

Dr. June's Education:

Bachelor's Degree in Public Relations at Austin Peay State University

Master's Degree in Corporate Communications at APSU. While in Graduate School at APSU, Dr. June studied in London (Winter 2011/2012) and studied under the top three global marketing/advertising/communication firms in the world. She wrote a 20-page research paper comparing how the United Kingdom markets a product versus the United States. Dr. June completed the class with a grade of 100! Following graduation, she turned that paper into her first book, *Mark of the Beast*.

- One year of studies at World Harvest Bible College
- Doctor of Theology at International Miracle Institute

Prior to this book, she has written sixteen books. This is the seventh book of the *What the World?* Series. These books will help the Bride to understand the end-time events taking place and to prepare for Heaven.

Made in the USA
Las Vegas, NV
07 May 2022

48576238R00115